Through the Landscape of Faith

Through the Landscape of Faith

Lucy Bregman

The Westminster Press
Philadelphia

© 1986 Lucy Bregman

Scripture quotations from the Revised Standard Version of the Bible are copyrighted 1946, 1952, © 1971, 1973 by the Division of Christian Education of the National Council of the Churches of Christ in the U.S.A. and are used by permission.

Grateful acknowledgment for permission to reprint is made to:

Harcourt Brace Jovanovich, Inc., for an excerpt from "Little Gidding" in *Four Quartets* by T. S. Eliot, copyright 1943 by T. S. Eliot; renewed 1971 by Esme Valerie Eliot.

New American Library, for Canto XXXIII, lines 85–87, from *The Paradiso* by Dante, translated by John Ciardi (1970).

Book design by Gene Harris

First edition

Published by The Westminster Press®
Philadelphia, Pennsylvania

PRINTED IN THE UNITED STATES OF AMERICA

9 8 7 6 5 4 3 2 1

Library of Congress Cataloging-in-Publication Data

Bregman, Lucy.
  Through the landscape of faith.

  Bibliography of Christian initiation literature: p.
  1. Christian life—1960–   I. Title.
BV4501.2.B694   1986   248.4   85-26381
ISBN 0-664-24704-0 (pbk.)

Contents

Acknowledgments

My thanks and appreciation to

My colleagues at Temple University, especially Dr. Gerard S. Sloyan;

My brothers and sisters in Christ at Living Word Community, especially Ms. Helen LaFarge Mesick;

and to other friends who have provided support and guidance when needed, especially Steve and Roxie Dunning.

Do you not know that all of us who have been baptized into Christ Jesus were baptized into his death? We were buried therefore with him by baptism into death, so that as Christ was raised from the dead by the glory of the Father, we too might walk in newness of life.

—Romans 6:3–4

> And the end of all our exploring
> Will be to arrive where we started
> And know the place for the first time.

—T. S. Eliot, "Little Gidding"

I go now to him whom I saw in baptism.

—A dying East African woman

Introduction:
Baptism as Beginning Place
in the Christian Landscape

"Who am I in Christ?" I wonder. I cannot before God answer this question by avoiding my actual lived history as an adult person. I can have no fictitious spiritual autobiography apart from this real history. For most Christians, baptism lies far in the past and is barely an event in their remembered lives. Yet because baptism stands as a beginning place of Christian life, it can indeed become a beginning place in the deepest sense, a source of true identity and a point from which to view one's own unique past, present, and future. The question "Who am I in Christ?" may be answered, I believe, by connecting the basic imagery of baptism with each person's lived individual experience of newness, hope, and meaning. To find such meaning through faith in Christ is to participate in God's great project of redemption. I will then live out within my own self and among my neighbors the same experiences to which the Bible bears witness.

For many adults today, making this autobiographical connection between the realities of Christian faith and their own actual lives is very difficult. It has always been so, if the connection is to be real and not superficial. In this book, I try to connect the language of baptism as the rite of Christian beginning with themes of meaning and identity. I draw heavily from psychology, for where else have so many modern persons turned for insight into their own lives? Yet I believe the baptismal imagery of joining Christ in death and resurrection can become accessible to those of us steeped in psychology. For baptism's theme is the person as "new birth" and as participant in what happened to Christ. Through these images, the baptized are challenged to change their frame of reference about themselves. Even when baptism took place long before one's earliest conscious memories, its imagery has power to bring purpose out of confusion, hope out of despair, and life out of death.

While working recently on a major but finally unsuccessful academic project on baptism, I was deeply engrossed in problems of identity in Christ and the nature of the personal past. During the three years I strove to complete this project, I began to learn the paradox beneath Paul's clear declarations that "our old self was crucified with him" and "we have died with Christ." I began to recognize how, despite all the imagery of "new birth" and "new creation" a Christian may use, the past remains; it is not obliterated. It continues to abide within us, retaining its hold until it can be brought into relation with Jesus Christ's living power. The redemption of the past, not its obliteration: Is this what the death language of the Bible signifies? Is this what baptismal imagery points toward? If so, how do I appropriate such meanings in my own life?

Here I found my own previous theological preferences challenged. It was as if the Lord seemed to do everything possible to stress to me his power, healing, and deliverance, the working out of his redemption, in a practical and positive way. I had previously admired theologies that gave Christians a choice between a superficial optimistic vending-machine God and a real God of weakness and suffering. My own choice was different: that between a God who really can redeem, and wants to do so, and one who is remote and indifferent. The living God of the New Testament was and is no vending machine, promising health, wealth, and happiness at the push of a button. But to discard all imagery of divine power (as I had been inclined to do) is to falsify the gospel, which promises resurrection and newness of life.

I scrapped my original plan and began another book on baptism, this one closer to the marrow of what had really excited me all along. This book, the present one, is conceived as a work on the role of baptismal imagery in Christian autobiography, in the task given all of us of constructing our "life maps." I want to explore the meaning of baptism's imagery—essential inner meaning, not accidental meaning—in the context of lived individual Christian experience. This imagery tells us that we have both a death and a new beginning. How can one look upon one's own history, one's lived autobiography, in the light of this imagery? What becomes of one's past, and to what goal does baptismal language point? The ultimate context here will be baptismal imagery as it structures the Christian's relation to Christ, as this affects one's past and present, one's beginning and ultimate end. This is the stuff of both my experience and my scholarship.

A work using this method and dealing with lived Christian experiencing cannot be written at arm's length from its author's personal history. So although this book on life maps and baptism is in no way my own spiritual autobiography, there are a few things I ought to say about myself of a directly autobiographical nature. I became a Christian through conversion and was baptized at the age of thirty-four; thus my obvious affinity for models of baptismal spirituality developed in the ancient church with adult converts in mind. Yet I would describe myself as an evangelical Christian whose piety is structured more by the Bible than by the later liturgical developments of the church. Therefore, my approach to baptism and its imagery is guided more directly by the New Testament perspectives than by the images of the church fathers who spoke so eloquently on the subject.

I had been a religion scholar before my conversion, and in my scholarship I focused on nontraditional manifestations of religious life in the midst of supposedly secular society and forms of knowledge. Contemporary psychology especially fascinated me for its seeming ability to function religiously for so many modern persons. To become a Christian required a shift in attitude toward both this material and my own previous ways of studying it. Yet it did not mean either giving up scholarship in itself or completely rejecting the voices of contemporary psychology. These voices cannot be ignored; they speak in an idiom which is still mine and which I share with many educated persons today. Whether or not they speak truly, adequately, or even helpfully, there is no denying that they speak plausibly. Psychology, the questions it raises and the frameworks it provides, remains for me a kind of native language, as the tongue of classical theology will never be. Consequently, the ongoing back-and-forth dialectic between biblical images and psychological theories, which occupies so much of this nontraditional book on baptism, is drawn from an internal dialogue between the same voices. It is only fair to say that the odd combination of being a born-again Christian and having a scholarly background in the study of religion and psychology has probably amused and bemused my friends and colleagues—and myself as well.

But if this work is no spiritual autobiography, it is also not a sociological or historical study of how baptism as a rite of Christian initiation has developed down through the centuries. Rather, I am fascinated by the role of the beginning place in Christian soul-making, in that pilgrimage through life most often imagined in simple linear terms but, I believe, not most truly apprehended by such a model. As all three quotations placed at the start of this book suggest, the beginning and the end share an eternal bond, which stands at the heart of all that lies between. This bond allows for the continuing presence of the past, as well as the elusive in-breaking of the future. For Christian experience, it is the personal Lord Jesus Christ who is and makes real that bond, the One in whom these and all other things are held whole. The set of temporal-spiritual relations established in baptism is the true subject of this work.

1
Adult Faith and Life-Mapping

Imagine a wide sun-scorched desert, with no source of water or shade in sight. Imagine yourself one of many isolated lost wanderers, seeking liquid to drink and a shelter against the heat. You see, far off in the distance, something that shimmers green —just on the horizon, it seems. Is it an oasis or a mirage? You have no way to tell from where you stand, but also nothing to lose by trying to march toward it. The desert sun sweeps down murderously, and you tread slowly toward the goal, at the edge of your vision. From here, you cannot tell if it is real. You keep walking, using up your strength and body moisture as you go. If you are walking toward an oasis, there will be a well; there will be shade and people to care for you. If you are tracking a mirage, you will die of thirst as surely as if you'd stayed where you were. The shape on the horizon seems a little closer but not much . . . and you still can't be sure it is a real oasis and not an illusion. But by now you have no choice, only hope. There is no point in turning back.

You draw closer. Your mouth is dry and your eyes hurt from the glare. Yes, there is something there: trees, stone houses! At last you stagger into a tiny green circle of life. There, in the center, is a fountain. You reach its edge and plunge your hands into it and drink. You bathe your head in the water. Yes, this is a real oasis! It is no mirage. You have found a place of beauty, life, and peace in the middle of the desert. You want to shout to any other wanderers, "Hey, there's water here!"

This allegory may not describe everyone's experience in seeking a connection between the Living Lord of the Christian gospel and one's own lived existence. Yet for me, and I believe for many, this is what coming to Christian faith seems like. For some, the whole landscape of Christian spiritual geography is completely foreign territory, for which our presuppositions and cultural values fail to prepare us. These create some of the distance between ourselves and the oasis. For others, whose chief recollections of Christianity are the flannel-board Jesus or unpleasant experiences in Sunday schools or church camps, the desert quest is made worse by these dismal memories. For either group, to seek to discover the Living Water of Christ in mid-adulthood will involve a tough struggle against the resistances we bring as persons with formed identities. We seek as ones with histories of compromise with our own ideals, histories of being enmeshed in evil, and some recognition that the world we have built for ourselves is indeed a vast desert. Thus we seek amid obstacles—emotional, cultural, spiritual. And the promise of the allegory is that, yes, there is something thirst-quenching out there. It is no mirage or illusion based on wishful thinking; it is a variant of the ancient promise that "every one who asks receives, and he who seeks finds, and to him who knocks it will be opened" (Luke 11:10).

The exhausting trek across a dismal desert landscape is not the final or most accurate image of what happens when someone begins an inward appropriation of Christian teachings, values, images. For after we find the water at the oasis fountain, the picture changes. The truer picture is that we are not the first to seek; even while we are wanderers in the desert, God is searching for us. He leaps the mountains to come to us, running to meet us with arms open to embrace us. Once the search is over, we can recognize that many of the journey's hardships were, in fact, of our own making, and the struggle through them is not therefore so heroic as we might have thought. Paradoxically, it is even as much a flight as a quest—although we never would have seen it that way at the time.

And yet, in spite of that, the image of the desert quest retains some validity after all. For as one living in the late twentieth century, I ask my questions in terms of meaning, self-actualization, identity. I am not seeking "salvation" but saving, revitalizing life. I do not seek "justification" and "sanctification" but a relationship with God that will give my life an inner coherence and vitality that I lack. Because of this difference in emphasis, the technical vocabulary of much traditional Christianity appears as a foreign language to me. Or, to avoid too much reliance on the metaphor of translation, traditional Christianity seems to have been developed by and for men and women whose problems were substantially different from mine. A simple question such as "What must I do to be saved?" is distant from the questions I initially ask. I must, I feel, travel across miles of rock and sand before the question even makes sense to me, before I can ask it as *my* question.

Moreover, as a living human being I never encounter "Christianity" but primarily Christian people, never "the church" but people who comprise particular expressions of the church. The foreignness of the language is often mixed with a set of even more foreign and seemingly bizarre expectations about persons. In spite of all assurances to the contrary, Christians often manage to give the impression that theirs is a religion for perfect people. Although perfection may not be required upon entrance, it will be considered the standard very soon afterward. And the model of a "saved," redeemed person, although it varies from community to community, is often one where innocence and inexperience play major roles. Current emphasis on newness and transformation augments this; I shall call this "the myth of the fresh start" and measure it against the implications of the biblical images usually cited to authorize it. "My sister was very nearly a prostitute," confided one young man, "and now she's a sweet little Christian girl." Perhaps. A fresh start. But to enter the kingdom of God as a little child does not—or ought not—require that my model for a Christian identity remain at the level of childishness and unreality that the phrase "a sweet little Christian girl" evokes.

Now these two problems are most often treated as separable, however intermingled they may be in experience. The first—the essential foreignness of traditional Christian language and imagery—often leads directly to remarks on the secularity of "modern man," on the supposedly mythological and prescientific character of the Bible and the supposed impossibility for modern persons to have faith in its teachings. But modern persons have not proved as secular as many thinkers who worried about the problem predicted, if by "secular" one means uninvolved with religious language and concerns of any kind. There are, in fact, numerous ways to be religious—and even "mythological"—in today's setting. Some of these ways rely on language that is deliberately contemporary, deliberately relevant, language that seems designed to deliver the saving water of the oasis without the long trek across the desert. Some of this language is used by Christians, in a well-intentioned effort to remove unnecessary obstacles for those who seek.

Substitutions that try to bypass or omit this travel fail. They fail not because they are no longer biblical in some simplistic sense but because they are drawn from our own agendas. Sooner or later, the Living Lord will bring home to us that these agendas are faulty. The desert trip, representing the distance between my agenda and his, will always be a part of my Christian life. If I substitute "What must I do to find health and meaning in my life?" for "What must I do to be saved?" I will eventually discover that the way to reach these goods is to follow Christ through to Calvary. This path displaces and negates all my ideas of health and most of my preconceptions about meaning. Eventually, the substitute forms of the original question somehow fail to do justice to the One who answers it, and who is himself the answer. They fail to let God be God in all his mystery, complexity, and power.

But if the first problem requires that I let God be God, the second problem—unrealistic models of what "saved" persons are to be like—requires that God let me be me, and not a cardboard copy of my own or someone else's ideal of a perfect person. Ironically, those Christians who have been most adamant and faithful in preserving the full foreignness of traditional language have been among the most enthusiastic advocates of flattened, insipid, or grossly oversimplified models of saved or redeemed persons. The same God whose majesty, power, and infinite love are proclaimed redeems us from sin, death, and darkness only to make of us "sweet little Christian girls" and their masculine counterparts, athletic, wholesome, youthful Mr. Insipids. Such persons may indeed exist, but the task of adult identity is grossly distorted when they are made the standard. There is a sense in which this ideal is also a way not to let God be God; implicitly, at least, there is the fear that real adults with real adult problems are too much for him to handle.

The task of life-mapping is the task of discerning a coherent whole in the multiplicity of one's experiences. One necessary first step is to abandon images of "sweet little Christian girls" that mistake innocence and inexperience for redeemed humanity. Whatever the newness of life provided by baptism's power might imply, it ought not to drive us to this false exclusion of adult identity. Even the models of the myth of the fresh start I will discuss in chapter 5 will not be identical with such cardboard ideals; such models are speaking as and for adults. As an adult, I desperately need a life map; as a Christian, I even more desperately require a vision of a life redeemed, converted to Christ. This requires a God whom I let be God, a Christ utterly different from the flannel-board Jesus of Sunday schools, and an acknowledgment of adulthood in all its ambiguities. Here, the voices of various contemporary psychologies, as well as traditional spiritualities, join in offering a variety of models for the kind of life map I require.

In this book, I explore one beginning place for such a life map —or, rather, for several styles of Christian life maps. What is required is, perhaps, a beginning place in the world of imagination, of imagery. In one sense, our starting places are the questions we start with—questions about meaning and health, about inner coherence or lack of it in our own lives. But these are deceptive and misleading as beginning places. What is needed is a true beginning place, a reality rooted in the realm of Christian faith and also—potentially—in our own apprehension and experience of our selves.

Baptismal imagery is selected as one such beginning place. One reason is that baptism begins Christian life in the most obvious sense of being its starting point in time. It is, and always has been, the major rite of Christian beginning or initiation into the Christian community, as we shall see in the next chapter. But it is also a rite that all kinds of Christians share, something Protestants and Catholics, evangelicals and liberals, mystics and social activists all have undergone. But primarily, for us, it will be a beginning place in another sense: Its imagery holds a key to how the link with Christ the Lord restructures one's life, one's total history as it is lived and experienced. The imagery of baptism, not the rite itself, is the entrance into that landscape of faith we will call "spiritual geography."

One explanation might be needed as to the view of the Bible, and the use to be made of it, in the pages that follow. The New Testament is not—thank God!—a manual about baptism. It is not a manual or how-to-do-it book about anything, although it includes many materials with this intention. To be a biblical Christian means, I believe, to recognize this fact and let the Bible—both Old and New Testaments—be itself: a gloriously unsystematic anthology of a people's encounter with God, through whose words that same God is truly present and accessible to us.

The Bible as Christians have it is not the Talmud—which is indeed an encyclopedia-length how-to-do-it book for Orthodox Jews. Nor, at the other extreme, is it much like the Chinese Taoist scripture *Tao Te Ching,* a work of enigmatic poetic beauty that contains nothing resembling practical instruction with regard to marriage, property disputes, or public worship. Because the Bible is not very much like the Talmud, it is impossible to draw from its text absolutely unambiguous answers to every question that has ever perplexed Christians through the centuries. As we shall see, this has certainly been the case for some of the specific concerns regarding baptism. But because the Bible is not the *Tao Te Ching* either, it makes sense to investigate what it *does* have to say on the subject. And it speaks on many levels. Sometimes the practices of the earliest Christians stand as normative; sometimes we may wonder if what counts is not whatever they did but what they and we ought to be doing in light of the deepest intentions of the gospel.

For some who describe themselves as "biblical Christians" this outlook may sound far too fuzzy and mushy. It makes no reference to "inerrancy" or "infallibility" or any of the other terms often used in debates about biblical authority. But let me reassure such folk on one crucial point. All credible thought on baptism, its imagery, and its oft-debated function as Christian initiation takes the New Testament as authoritative. It is also important that all the New Testament authors took the Hebrew scriptures as authoritative. What this means is that a view of baptism that began and ended with an anthropologist's view of initiation ritual or a psychologist's view of child development would be judged defective by every contemporary Christian scholar.

At the same time, in this context to take the Bible as authoritative cannot mean merely to restate its most mysterious, profound, and evocative passages without some attempt to link them explicitly to our own life experiences and styles of thought. To take the Bible seriously as authoritative implies that this process of apprehension, appropriation, and existential encounter is intrinsic to our interpreting its images, narratives, and directives.

For the Bible itself acts as a kind of oasis on the horizon, as in our allegory. Its narratives and images, its theological reflections and poetry, invite us, in the words of Karl Barth,

> to reach for the last highest answer, in which all is said that can be said, although we can hardly understand and only stammeringly express it. And that answer is: A new world, the world of God.[1]

To speak of a Christian life map, or of spiritual geography, is to express this entrance into "the world of God," a landscape foreign to the one we have known and existing in perpetual tension with it. How this world of God becomes our world, its geography the inner plan for our autobiography, our soul-making, is what this book is all about.

2
Baptismal Imagery and Christian Experience

The term "Christian initiation" is a current one and includes all those rites and processes by which a person becomes joined to Christ's body, the church. Most discussions of baptism begin and end from exactly this perspective and are directed at church leaders, who must set policies on whom to baptize, whom to rebaptize, and whom not to baptize. Seldom is the viewpoint of the baptized person introduced into the discussion, and then usually as evidence in support of some general guideline for church practice. To this day, nonscholarly discussions of baptism among ordinary Christians follow this format and center on the question, "Should we have our baby daughter baptized, or wait until she is old enough to know what baptism is about and want it for herself?" In this chapter, I will survey the New Testament roots for baptism's meaning, first in the light of these normal concerns of practice. Then I will show how baptism's inner meaning, especially in Paul and the Fourth Gospel, leads into different questions, to issues of personal life-structuring. In this context, the relation between baptism and conversion becomes important. What I will stress is the rite's imagery, and less the sacrament itself.

Before I begin, one point upon which all now agree should be made: Paul and the other New Testament writers addressed adult converts, and for several centuries adult conversion and baptism was the statistical norm. When reminded of baptism as the place of new birth, of death to sin and to the old self, these converts could remember the day of their baptism and what they had felt during the rite. Nevertheless, how primary should we make this appeal to personal memory? Paul never wrote, "Don't you remember what you experienced when you were baptized?" but "Do you not know that all of us who have been baptized into Christ Jesus were baptized into his death?" (Rom. 6:3). Thus baptism is a beginning place where something happens in spiritual geography, to our inmost self. Our old self dies, nailed to the cross and enclosed in Christ's tomb. A new self is brought into being, born from above, raised up by God to be free from the powers of sin and death. Baptism is the inward beginning place, and like all beginning places it can serve for reflection on self, death, past, and future, as these are made new in Christ. To play this role, baptism need not always be a personal memory. It can be a spiritual fact, a point of entrance into life in Christ, even in the absence of specific memories of one's own baptism.

Today, a thorough answer to even the prosaic question "Should our baby be baptized?" returns us to the foundations of baptism, its basic meaning. The writings on baptism as Christian initiation send the reader to the New Testament and the practices of the early church, as guides for how baptism ought to be viewed today. The New Testament, while it may not provide one and only one doctrine of baptism or set of answers to specific practical questions, does offer certain fundamental frameworks for thinking about the rite and its meaning. And the New Testament and other ancient materials allow for far more attention to the experience of baptized persons than do most of today's discussions.

What did the New Testament church believe baptism to be, and why did it baptize its new members? The rite derives from the practice of John "the baptizer" as a ritual of repentance to prepare for the eschatological reign of God. "Eschatological" refers to the end time, when God will save his people and bring history to a close. John's practice was intended for the renewal of Israel, so that all obstacles to the mighty work of God would be removed. Jesus' participation in John's rite was seen by the early church as the fulfillment of this hope. Therefore, the followers of Jesus simply continued the external rite—immersion in water—while adding many layers of new meaning to it. The new meanings were congruent with the original one, and "Repent and be baptized!" continued as a Christian exhortation.

Christians, however, made one basic addition: Their baptism

was performed in the name of Jesus. To do any act "in the name of" someone creates a bond between the person directly involved in that act and the one in whose name it is performed. Scholars have coined the term "corporate personality" to express the idea behind this belief. Corporate personality implies that one's identity is found not in one's unique individuality but in the family, the community, or the suprapersonal unit. This may have been the normal mode of identity for most people of the Old Testament. Therefore, to act in the name of someone will create a real, not fictitious, bond wherein the corporate or communal selfhood becomes primary. In other words, Jesus becomes the true identity of the Christian baptized in his name. Unfortunately, for us this is hard to grasp, for a term such as "identity" implies "unique individuality" in our psychological concepts. Our very language about persons depends on a much more individualized sense of selfhood.

Baptism in the name of Jesus was the rite of entrance into the movement composed of Jesus' followers, those who not only acknowledged him as Lord and Christ but sensed him as a living presence among and within them. This view makes it plain that no one is baptized in total isolation from the church, Christ's body. And however diverse the churches of the New Testament era may have been, "one Lord, one faith, one baptism" expressed a sense of being part of one enterprise.

The account of Pentecost in Acts implicitly portrays another aspect of baptism. The church begins with the "pouring out" of the Holy Spirit, as an eschatological event. Baptism in water for Christians was linked to baptism in the Spirit—although, as certain episodes in Acts show, the two could be separated. However, the normal view was that at baptism the new Christian received the Holy Spirit, the invisible power and presence of God, to abide within him or her and be shared by all members of the group. "To live according to the Spirit" and to act "through the power of the Spirit" were directives aimed at all Christians by virtue of their baptism. It is impossible to tell whether the watery image of "poured-out Spirit" in Joel 2:28–29 helped make firm this connection between a rite of repentance involving water and the sense of empowerment expressed by many references to "the Spirit in us." These meanings for baptism appear to have been shared throughout the churches of the New Testament era.

In contrast, the Pauline and Johannine imagery of baptism, of which we will have much to say, was not at first so universal. The emphasis in Paul is on making "corporate personality" an inner reality, so that in baptism "that which happened to Christ happens also to Christians."[1] The primary happenings are no longer Jesus' own baptism but his death, burial, and resurrection. These "Christ events" were then to be worked out in every area of the Christian's personal and social existence. They provide a paradigm for identity and action "in Christ."

Likewise, another interiorizing of baptism began in the church(es) associated with the name of John the Evangelist. This was birth from "water and the Spirit," an idea that became influential in later centuries, until it dominated the liturgy of the ancient church. In the Fourth Gospel, the image makes its appearance not in Jesus' encounter with John the baptizer but as part of the discourse with Nicodemus—which, like much of John's Gospel, is filled with complex dualities. Born from Spirit vs. born from flesh, ascent and descent, heavenly vs. earthly things, knowledge vs. ignorance: It is far from obvious how directly this language refers to baptism, although it seems a meditation on the rite's inner meaning.[2]

Baptism involved not only freedom from past sin but freedom in future from the power of sin, through the presence of the Holy Spirit within the baptized Christian. The ancient church's standards for who should be baptized were high, but those for postbaptismal conduct even higher. The really serious problem became how to deal with postbaptismal sin. Who could hope to live a sin-free postbaptismal life? This must have intimidated a large number of persons, especially those who (like the emperor Constantine) served in positions of public power requiring morally ambiguous actions. The New Testament provided no one clear directive for handling this problem. Its writings include the advice to confess our sin (1 John 1:9) in confident expectation of God's forgiveness, but also the flat statement "For if we sin deliberately after receiving the knowledge of the truth, there no longer remains a sacrifice for sins, but a fearful prospect of judgment" (Heb. 10:26–27). The problem of church discipline this created led to rites of postbaptismal cleansing, the sacrament of penance. But baptism's power could be made to work forward in time as well as backward. By virtue of one's baptism, one can anticipate God's forgiveness if one sins and then repents.

Baptism as Christian initiation became controversial during the Reformation. Two major debates over baptism surfaced at that time and have remained sources of contention ever since. The first of these is whether baptism should indeed be considered a sacrament, using the Roman Catholic definition of a sacrament as "the visible sign of invisible grace." Or is faith in Christ what counts for salvation? The second issue is that of believers' baptism vs. the baptism of infants. The former is far less likely to give rise to direct disputes today, for scholars both Catholic and Protestant recognize that the New Testament bound faith and baptism together as later theologies did not. To ask "faith or baptism?" is to ask an entirely bizarre question of the New Testament writers. In the words of Roman Catholic scholar Rudolf Schnackenburg:

> Faith and baptism belong together, but they are at all times significant in themselves. . . . Baptism without faith in Christ is unimaginable for the thought of the primitive church.[3]

Baptism was never a mere ritual, performed in obedience to Christ's command but without internal and specific reason. For Baptist scholar G. R. Beasley-Murray,

> God's gracious giving to faith belongs to the context of baptism, even as God's gracious giving in baptism is to faith. . . . Faith therefore ought not to be represented as self-sufficient; Christ comes to it in the Gospel, in the sacraments.[4]

If the New Testament itself provides the subtle and holistic relation between faith and baptism, this ought to invite contemporary Protestants and Catholics to overcome the dismal disputes of the past.

But this solution, that "faith and baptism belong together," leads right to the heart of the other area of conflict for baptism as Christian initiation. If it is true that "baptism without faith in Christ is unimaginable for the thought of the primitive church," it has certainly been "imaginable" at other points in Christian history. Here, however, the theological and the historical issues need to be carefully separated. "Did the early church baptize infants?" is one kind of question. "Should they have, and should we?" is another. The answer to the first question is, I believe, impossible to determine.[5] The second question, however, must be answered—and most of today's literature on Christian initiation addresses it.

Should infants and those without personal, experiential faith in Christ be baptized? The most relevant and often-cited arguments on behalf of infant baptism today include the following:

1. Baptism is like circumcision, a rite of initiation into the people of God, where the faith of the community is what counts.

2. Faith is not an intellectual affirmation but an attitude of trust, which an infant may share, even if he or she cannot articulate it clearly.

3. It is ridiculous to treat the children of believers as being on a par with "pagans"; such an attitude falsifies their situation. When combined with the first, this third argument provides a powerful rationale for the baptism of infants whose parents exhibit real faith in Christ.

Although Augustine's rationale for baptism as cleaning from "original sin" plays no explicit role in these arguments, one wonders if infant baptism would have been begun and developed as a norm for practice without it.

Against the baptizing of infants and very young children, one finds today the following arguments:

1. Baptism goes together with repentance; an infant cannot repent.

2. "Faith" really does include a mental affirmation, for "faith in Christ" is not just an attitude of shapeless trust. Therefore infantile "faith" is not meaningful and cannot be sufficient for baptism.

3. If in the age of Christendom being a baptized Christian was almost a universal fate, that is clearly no longer the case today. To be a Christian is a voluntary individual commitment, and baptismal practice should correspond to this situation.

In actual practice, which of these arguments prevails depends upon many factors, with official theologies of baptism being only one—and often not the primary one. Surely the authority of Karl Barth (who opposed infant baptism) has been forced on occasion to yield to pressure from pious grandparents. Equally, the lack of pious grandparents may have made more plausible the view of the church as a voluntary association of committed individuals rather than an organic unity of families.

However, what strikes me in this debate is not the strength and validity of the arguments but how little attention is given to what the sacrament really means for Christians at the deepest level of their lived existence. Somehow it is much easier to remain with questions of church policy than to explore the insight raised by the words of the dying Christian, "I go now to him whom I saw in baptism." These reveal unexplored, uncharted territory, the inner landscape of baptism's meaning.

To explore this landscape, we must repeat that the basic baptismal imagery of the New Testament was developed with adults in mind. Not just repentance but the other themes of baptism fit the experiences of adult converts. Even today, the powerful experiences of some adult converts provide evidence for just how meaningful baptism can be when it indeed coincides with repudiating an old identity and taking on a new. It is *this* dimension of baptism—as experience structured by imagery—that really enables it to function for life-mapping: for us too, not merely for the Christians of the ancient church. Themes such as "corporate personality" and "new birth" find their fulfillment in the personal experiences of Christians, then and now. And so we can return to the writings of the New Testament to find in them a vision of "death to the old self" and "newness of life" that lies at the core of Christian identity. With this in mind, let us see again what Paul and the Gospel of John say about baptism as imaged experience.

Pauline baptismal references, and the theology of baptism Paul developed, evoke the perspective of the baptized person. Paul writes as a church leader but as one who, along with his readers, is included in "all of us" who were baptized. The kind of questions that interest him are those connecting baptism to the whole of Christian experience. Although it is common to speak of Paul's "theology of baptism," most of what he says proceeds by means of a few striking images. Specifically, for Paul baptism is our crucifixion, death, and burial with Christ, and also—with reservations—our resurrection with him. The central images are death and resurrection: first Christ's, then our own. This imagery raises several questions about its import for individual Christian experiencing today. However, our account of it omits a detailed study of Pauline theology or of all the historical and textual problems scholars have uncovered and debated.[6]

Paul, it seems, accepted the fact of baptism as a rite of Christian initiation. He did nothing to abandon or change its outward form. Schnackenburg, a thorough scholarly expositor of Pauline baptism, argues that the apostle's liturgical interest was minimal.[7] Nevertheless, he could connect baptism with what mattered most in his own spiritual life: precisely the awareness that that life was no longer his but Christ's. To be baptized was to participate in Christ's death, to join him in the tomb. This required the crucifixion of "the sinful body," the old, pre-Christian self. To be baptized was to share what happened to Christ. And so, just as God had raised Christ from death, the Christian too was to become "alive to God" and "walk in newness of life" (Rom. 6:3–11). Paul could use this view of baptism to address specific issues, such as the quality of life in the Spirit. He used the motif of baptismal oneness in Christ to obliterate Jew–Gentile distinctions in the church. Baptism was not an isolated topic for him but, rather, integrated into a total vision of Christian life.

Pauline baptism was also an eschatological act, one whose fulfillment points toward the day of Christ, the time of God's consummation. Paul's eschatology is, in the language of biblical scholarship, "unrealized." (In contrast, "realized eschatology" focuses on the fulfillment made available *now* through Christ.) The resurrected Christ is the first fruit of a general resurrection, to occur in the future. This lies ahead in the "not yet," the last day. This is the day toward which God is moving, for which all creation groans. Paul too awaited it. He expected the return of Christ and the complete triumph of God, a state when God will be "everything to every one" (1 Cor. 15:28). Therefore, what Christians could experience now, after Christ's resurrection and postbaptism, was still just a foretaste, an anticipation of this day of Christ.[8]

Paul's converts, on the other hand, had a tendency to see baptism as equal to full salvation. Baptism is a beginning, for Paul; it is never a guarantee of salvation, as it subtly becomes in more realized eschatologies. In Corinth, some converts apparently claimed, "We are baptized; therefore we are already fully saved and even fully 'resurrected.' Consequently, whatever we do cannot be sinful." They saw this logic as the proper outcome of baptism as death to the old sinful self. They could also take Paul's language of freedom from the law and interpret it according to this vision of baptism.

Paul's angry response leaves no doubt where he stood in regard to this line of thought. Although biblical scholar Christiaan Beker thinks that "incorporation language has a logic of its own,"9 Paul insisted that baptismal incorporation into Christ did not automatically guarantee salvation. But he never dismisses baptism as a "mere ritual"; instead, he reminds his converts, "But you were washed, you were sanctified, you were justified in the name of the Lord Jesus Christ and in the Spirit of our God" (1 Cor. 6:11). Baptism does change one's condition—therefore act as who you are, not who you were.

Were the mistakes made by the Corinthians as foolish as this summary (and most others) make them sound? Paul's language of "buried with Christ" and "new life in Christ" carries with it the sense of a new mode of existence beyond the limits that previously bound the self. If Paul really meant that the old self, subject to sin, dies and is buried with Christ in baptism, why should one not act so as to express one's contempt for the old, the restrictive, the law-bound? How much death and how much newness and resurrection was Paul himself committed to, and how much was he willing to tolerate in others? If incorporation language has its own internal logic, the imagery of death and resurrection does too. At what point does this logic collide with other claims? We may not literally repeat the mistakes of the Corinthians, but their confusion over the relation of new to old, and "now" to "not yet," will be a sign to us that remapping one's life experience has never been simple.

Now this issue arises in a different form in scholarly debates over Pauline authorship of Ephesians and Colossians. (These letters are often described today as Deutero-Pauline.) Why should this be? Because Paul's undisputed writings, including Romans and Corinthians, are all remarkably reserved in their use of resurrection language to describe the "now" of Christian life.10 Those who find Colossians and Ephesians Deutero-Pauline claim that the latter disregard the "historical" Paul's nervousness about too much resurrection language in the present evil age.11

It seems that behind the historical question of authorship lie two different visions of Christian experience. In some scholarly circles, "realized" eschatology has a negative connotation, for it appears too triumphant, too blind to the abiding reality of pain, death, and evil in this preconsummation existence. "Unrealized" eschatology, with its concern for the future, sees God's redemption as incomplete and allows for what one scholar calls "a crucial and mysterious 'dark' residue of suffering and death in God's created order that will be resolved only by the final resurrection of the dead in the glory of God."[12] It may therefore seem more socially radical, and so preferred over "realized" eschatology's celebration of the "now." But perhaps this is our problem, not Paul's. Twentieth-century experience—somber and dreadful as it is—makes this reminder of a residue crucial for us, if not for Paul or the early Christians.

I find it hard to see in Colossians a betrayal of the basic Pauline principle that "what happened to Christ happens to the Christian." Its author—whether the original apostle (the "historical" Paul) or another person who wrote in his name—took seriously the baptismal theme of incorporation into Christ. When he developed this into an image of baptismal resurrection with Christ, he furthered the theme of death to the past, to sin, to the flesh. And this is probably why the early church found these letters truly Pauline. It is this theme of participation in Christ that draws one toward baptism as a starting place for a revisioned life, as well as membership in an ongoing church.

These (perhaps) Deutero-Pauline writings share one feature with the undisputed Pauline letters. They almost completely disregard events in the precrucifixion career of Jesus.[13] Christ's suffering, death, burial, and being raised by God are the Christ happenings that really count, the "eternal events." The hymn cited by Paul in Philippians 2:5–11 puts these eternal events into a framework of descent–ascent, self-emptying and exaltation. Pauline Christology is so focused on death and resurrection that the status of the preincarnation, preexistent Christ is of no independent interest, nor can it directly be part of our incorporation into Christ. Absent too is the issue of Jesus' divine and human natures, which of course became the major concern a few centuries later. This, by the way, is one reason Paul can write of Christ, "The death he died he died to sin" (Rom. 6:10) and not to stop to ask how Jesus could ever have been subject to sin in the first place. Death, burial (a kind of final stage of death), and then resurrection by God—with "suffering" mentioned often in the context of Paul's own sufferings: These Christ events are what baptism is all about, where the Christian begins to "put on Christ." The old self is killed, the new self raised by God.

Given this vision of baptism in the name of Christ as the key to new identities for Christians, how does it relate to what we call conversion? Conversion ordinarily is taken to mean a memorable sudden transformation in which the individual is turned around from a life of opposition to God to a life of loving relatedness to him. Conversion has been redefined as a gradual growth process, but for the sake of clarity I will keep the more usual meaning. Do baptismal imagery and conversion as personal experience have an intrinsic relationship to each other?

Let us use the kind of experience depicted in the Acts narrative of Saul on the Damascus road as the paradigm for conversion— whatever the historical Paul underwent.[14] In essence, such an experience includes a repudiation of the old self and its ways as the person encounters Christ. This is followed by a definite fresh start, a new self. On the Damascus road, Saul is confronted by the risen Jesus and is blinded. But then the scales fall from his eyes; he returns to life and is baptized. This sequence conforms to the sequence of happenings in baptism: death and then new life, new identity. Saul became Paul. It is in this sense that conversion and baptism belong together; they share a basic structure. This would be the case even if one's conversion were to take place long after baptism. As to the Paul of the letters ("historical" Paul), he indeed died to his old self, the Pharisee, the enthusiast for the law, and counted all that he had lost as refuse. His new life, his new selfhood, was Christ's. Therefore, although his own remarks on his encounter with the resurrected Lord are enigmatic, the inner structural unity between conversion and baptism is retained throughout his letters.

Such an intrinsic tie between conversion and baptism also includes the sense of repentance, of "death to sin," which the early Christian call to "repent and be baptized!" conveyed. Rather than two separate and essentially unrelated demands, repentance and baptism are two modes of the same process: the death of the sinful self. Baptism is never, if I follow this logic, a pure promise of "new life." We are baptized into Christ's death, not immediately into his resurrection; his death becomes our own. There can be no walk in newness of life without this death, no new start without rejection of the past. In baptism, I do not shrug off the past or leave it behind; I nail it to the cross, renouncing its life in me. This death frees me from sin, and so "you also must consider yourselves dead to sin and alive to God in Christ Jesus."

This unity of repentance and baptism signifies a radical bond between each baptized Christian and Christ. Not "imitate," remember, or even "follow" Christ. No, in baptism I join Christ, on the cross and in the tomb and (if we allow Colossians to complete the sequence) in the heavenly places. The Pauline answer to the song's question, "Were you there when they crucified my Lord?" is "Yes, in baptism everyone is there, and in baptism we are all laid in the tomb with him and raised by God to a new and resurrected life." To be baptized means to dwell in these places, to experience Christ's painful and gruesome death as our own death to sin.

Just as in Paul's thought baptism is always understood under the imagery of death, so in the Fourth Gospel baptism is a "new birth," a "birth from above." Curiously, if we think of baptism as Christian initiation, as a beginning place, this imagery of birth appears far more natural and obvious. This is so, even if we disagree over whether the reference to "born of water and the Spirit" in John 3:5 is truly a sacramental reference, as the later church took it to be.

This conflict, however, continues today in both scholarly and popular circles. How sacramental must one's understanding of this image be? Does "new birth" refer to a personal religious experience and stand entirely apart from any internal connection to baptism?[15] It is certainly possible to read the language of "new birth" without finding in it such an intrinsic connection. "Unless one is born anew, he cannot see the kingdom of God" (John 3:3). This could refer to some entirely internal event in one's experience and not to baptism at all.

Today's Christians who call themselves "born again" take this approach. They cite this same verse and do so with no baptismal connotations whatsoever. For born-again Christians, life in Christ really begins when one has a conversion experience, takes Jesus as personal Lord and Savior, gives one's life to Christ, meets the Lord, is saved. All these expressions mean the same thing, and all are deliberately contrasted to "mere churchgoing," which the persons involved may have done all their lives. Only with an experience of being born again has Christ's injunction been fulfilled. To be baptized without such an inner event substitutes ritual for reality.

In sharp contrast, the tie between spiritual birth and baptism was embraced by the ancient church. Many ancient pastors and theologians found the Fourth Gospel's image ideal to describe the true function of baptism. Baptism as birth led to the image of "Mother Church" as a mythic figure in baptism's drama. To be born through baptism was to become a child of Mother Church. Water, womb, fertility all pervaded this imagery. But it also combined with spiritual self-denial or asceticism: birth from woman was impure and earthly, birth from Virgin Mother Church was just the opposite. Bishop Zeno, A.D. c.370, told his baptismal candidates:

> You are to be born, not by the ordinary rules of childbirth—mothers groaning in the pain of labor and bringing you into the miseries of this world, weeping, sullied and wrapped in sullied swaddling clothes—but exalting in joy, children of heaven, children free from sin.[16]

This birth language captures something that Christians with a strong sacramental outlook and their opponents can share: the sense of newness, "childlike" wonder, and dependence on God. Although Zeno and today's born-again Christians could agree on few other things, they could joyfully unite in this awareness. New life in Christ is joyful, undoing the hurts and guilts of the past by cleansing. It gives those who experience this a tremendous sense of hope. The God who can make all things new has done so with me!

Testimonies from ancient Christians reveal this sense of newness as they describe what baptism means to them. No doubt, for many adult converts of the early Christian centuries, baptismal rebirth or regeneration was an intense and vivid reality. For example, Cyprian describes his prebaptism wretchedness and his doubts about how to live freed from sin's power.

> But at last I made up my mind to ask for baptism. I went down into those life-giving waters, and all the stains of my past were washed

away. I committed my life to the Lord; he cleansed my heart and filled me with his Holy Spirit. I was born again, a new man. . . . Then, in a most marvelous way, all my doubts cleared up. I could now see what had been hidden from me before. I found I could do things that had previously been impossible.[17]

No born-again Christian could fail to identify with this language, while advocates of a sacramental approach could emphasize that faith in God's power comes through baptism. For ancient Christians like Cyprian, processes that we have divided were held whole.

Why do images of "new birth" and "death with Christ" work so powerfully, whether for a Cyprian or for someone today? "The action of the Holy Spirit" is one answer. Yes, but in the images themselves there are strong psychological factors at work. The Spirit may be active precisely through unconscious levels of memory and experience. It is clear that birth imagery has a tremendous capacity to evoke infancy and modes of experiencing proper to it. Infancy was a time of purity and wholeness. For Zeno, baptism is the occasion for a return to the watery womb of Mother Church, a return in sacrament which simply must have evoked levels of nostalgia for the intimacy and union of early experience. Birth imagery depends directly on the fact that at one time we were all babies.

But in Zeno's words, we were all once babies "sullied" and "weeping." For many psychoanalysts, the principal result of birth is birth trauma, a painful separation from the all-sufficient enclosed womb. Not so much the filth of birth as its anxiety makes this experience less than joyful and positive. In the fourth-century bishop's meditations, spiritual birth reevokes the goodness of first birth but, on a more conscious level, allows us all to repudiate the tears, traumas, and pain that went along with it.

But if these associations to early experience help make birth imagery so powerful, Paul's language about the relation between the "new self" and Christ contains its own links to lost childhood experience. Between Christ and the self, there is not so much an I-Thou relationship of two independent interacting persons as a link far closer, more intimate. The self who lives in Paul is "I," yet "not I but Christ"; this ambiguity is due not to the apostle's confusion but to the fact that language itself assumes that persons, like other "objects," are completely separate from the sub-

ject who speaks of them. But in infancy and its mode of experiencing we have a merger between self and world rather than
a clear division between person observing and thing observed.
The mother, or even the beloved toy, is united to the self in love
—a relatedness that empowers the self so as to make all later ties
possible. Paul's experience of Christ in himself, therefore, may
evoke a mode of experiencing basic to early childhood but repressed or lost to later adult consciousness. Such psychological
associations are insights into the reason certain imagery works
for human beings (whether in the ancient world or for us). Far
from reducing the language of birth or life in Christ to mere
infantile experience and degrading it, these ideas show how
baptism as new beginning could be so effective in linking an
adult fresh start with earliest memories.

Although by virtue of its extensive use in the ancient church,
as well as by psychoanalytic theory, baptism as birth might have
priority, I have emphasized the Pauline language as a point of
departure for an exploration of baptism's inner meaning. I want
—indeed, require—*both* images, both death-resurrection and
birth. I believe the Pauline image should be, for Christians, the
primary one, regardless of the popularity of "new birth" for
ancient converts or for those today. Although both images are
found in scripture, the basic reason is that death-resurrection is
more closely tied to Christ. The imperative to be "born again"
and the reference to water and the Spirit are more extrinsic to
the Living Lord than the connection Paul discerned between
baptism and Christ, where the baptized join in Christ's death,
burial, and resurrection. For Christians the deepest meaning of
baptism will be that which links the rite most intrinsically to
Christ. And since elsewhere in the Fourth Gospel there is an
indirect yet extraordinary link with baptism of just the intrinsic
kind Paul saw,[18] my reservation is not with the Johannine Gospel
as such but with the tendency of birth symbolism to wander far
from any direct tie with Christ—as in Zeno's exhortations it
surely does.

What consequences follow from seeing death-resurrection
rather than birth as the primary baptismal image? Crucifixion is
a gruesome and mutilating form of death. When in Colossians it
is associated with circumcision (2:11), the imagery brings physical wounding to mind. Although baptism as a rite is never itself

physically painful, its imagery must bear the weight of these associations with Christ's physical mutilation. Baptism must in some way remain a beginning place that includes pain, not solely one of peace and joy.

A second consequence is to loosen the link between baptismal imagery and the social-churchly role of baptism throughout most of Christian history. We need to remember that baptism has functioned for over a thousand years as a birth ritual for Western Christendom, as a rite of passage in the anthropologist's sense. Understandably, this life-cycle function gave the language of birth a kind of social priority. Every infant in Christendom was born twice: once of woman and then again of Mother Church. Today this is no longer the case. This social shift makes it far easier to think in terms of baptismal imagery rather than church policy—and, in turn, giving priority to the Pauline death-resurrection imagery helps further to free us from debates over "infants vs. believers."

Perhaps one way to avoid a dualistic either/or between death-resurrection or birth is to suggest that birth could have been—or could be now—developed imaginatively in a much more Pauline fashion than it was in the ancient church. Zeno's division between "natural" and "spiritual" births included an aesthetic and moral dualism implied in his description of each. Natural birth has plenty of pain, of course—but it was precisely Zeno's goal to eliminate such thoughts from birth language associated with baptismal spirituality. When Paul, on the other hand, used birth language at all, he spoke with his converts of being "in travail" (Gal. 4:19). "Travail" for them was one more aspect of Paul's ongoing experience of sharing Christ's sufferings, of being crucified with Christ. Perhaps a truly Pauline view of baptism as birth would allow the inclusion of pain imagery. It would reject Zeno's aesthetic repugnance which made "sullied" natural birth from women so repulsive to him. If ordinary birth is both pain and joy, then perhaps even the most spiritual birth is too.

For in no way are death symbolism and birth language absolute alternatives. Both are intrinsic to baptism, as rite of initiation and as source of Christian experience. Both work as images—meaning that both make it possible for me to apprehend some level of meaning and reality not captured in ordinary language, a level of meaning that requires imagery for its vehicle. Both may succeed, because what I am after is not one perfect theology of baptism but a means to enter Christian spiritual geography as a suitable beginning place for re-visioning one's life maps. I can close this discussion of the two prominent biblical imageries of baptism in the hope that they will both function to unlock otherwise hidden dimensions of Christian existence.

3
From Imagery to Application: Worldview, Life Maps, and Spiritual Geography

It is one thing to explore how baptism's imagery of death and resurrection with Christ, or of new birth, dramatically affected the Christians of the ancient church. But how can such images work for persons today? Without some personal appropriation, the images of Paul and the Fourth Gospel will remain forever in "Bibleland" or "liturgyland"—two territories walled off from the actual lives of anyone. Before I can discuss our appropriation of these images, I need to develop some concepts or frameworks for understanding religious imagery and individual lived existence. This theoretical interlude will prepare us for detailed study of ways to connect Christian images to patterns of personal experience.

Normally, according to commonsense definition, a religion is a system of explicit, consciously held beliefs, practiced rituals, and ethical norms, tied to membership in a special institution. When we speak of someone as "religious," we have in mind that person's involvement at the level of belief, practice, values, and group membership. But is religion in this sense derived from something more fundamental? Many scholars would say so. Behind the explicit sets of beliefs and so on ordinarily identified as religion is an implicit worldview, which is defined as a picture of the whole of reality. The symbols of a religion evoke and establish a world, a picture of how things are and how we ourselves should behave in its context. Clifford Geertz's definition of religion takes this approach and is worth citing:

A system of symbols which acts to establish powerful, pervasive, and long-lasting moods and motivations in [human beings] by

formulating conceptions of a general order of existence and cloth-
ing these conceptions with such an aura of factuality that the moods
and motivations seem uniquely realistic.[1]

A symbol can be either a visual image or a word or concept that
stands for a reality beyond itself.

It is possible to hold such a system of symbols without necessarily belonging to a religion in the more ordinary sense. Moreover,
it is even more possible that my lived, taken-for-granted system
of symbols (religion in Geertz's sense) will not entirely coincide
with my official, explicitly held religion. When this occurs, the
latent worldview's vision of existence almost always wins out
over the more overt officially taught doctrines of my religion in
the ordinary sense. To give one popular example, there is a long
tradition of official Christian ethical teachings on wealth. But
who would argue that in America the combined weight of Benja-
min Franklin, Horatio Alger, and others have created a gospel
of success so pervasive and persuasive that it overshadows the
more "official" Christian ethics for many persons?[2]

The emphasis of a theorist such as Geertz is on the fundamental human need for such a universal order of existence as religion, in his sense, provides. The atheist, the antitraditionalist,
requires and holds a worldview just as surely as does the devout.
Why? The term coined by another theorist holds the clue. For
Anthony Wallace, every culture and every person functioning in
a culture must have a "mazeway"—a map of reality—in order to
be guided by it through life's crises and mysteries: not—according to Wallace and others—to flee from these mysteries, para-
doxes, and anomalies but to learn to recognize them.[3] In times
of crisis, cultural and personal, the mazeway must be resynthe-
sized, remapped. The worldview must be reconstructed in order
to make room for new experiences.

This use of worldview presupposes a certain understanding of
reality. "Reality" is not simply a given, an X "out there" waiting
to be discovered through objective means—as all of us initially
assume. This beginner's idea of reality is labeled "naive realism"
in philosophical discussion and is vigorously rejected by most
social scientists, including Geertz. Instead, what I apprehend as
reality is in part my own creation, a product of my synthesizing,
interpreting, and map-making activity. Yet such theories as

Geertz's are *not* solipsistic; they do not claim "I alone am real." There is indeed something "out there." But my apprehension of it is a far more active and engaged process than a mere reception of sense data. I need maps even to perceive—as I will discuss in more detail in regard to remembering.

Even the most rigid worldview is open to corrections from whatever lies "out there." We must not think of a worldview, a map, as a tyrannical force bent on imposing itself at all costs and withstanding all correction or change. My relationship with reality requires flexibility and adaptability and thus a worldview that can indeed make sense of things. The theories of religion that emphasize worldview or any similar concept do not imply that maps of reality are defensive, lying illusions against which the authentic or enlightened person must struggle.[4]

If worldview is basically a legacy of my culture, what is my own individual share in it? The worldview may provide the basic categories and assumptions that I accept mostly without thought, but my individual appropriation of them will not be identical with that of anyone else. In fact, each of us carries our own version of the cultural mazeway, amending it to suit our unique situation. And one very crucial aspect of this personalized worldview will be my own portrait of my self, my life as it unfolds in time, and my place in the universal order of meanings. This is what in chapter 1 I called a "life map." It is never simply a replication of the worldview, but it is always indebted to and derived from it.

In every society, just as there is a worldview, so individual persons require life maps. However, in a culture committed to a version of corporate personality such as that of the ancient Hebrews, life maps will be more alike and reveal far more overlap. They will be concerned with the individual largely as an instance of a typical member of the family, clan, tribe, people. Yet such persons still share in the task known as "the biographical process."[5] They too construct portraits of who they are, what their origin and destiny are, and how they as individuals fit within the larger systems of community and in the world as a whole. Their task may be simpler than mine, but it is a difference in degree and not in kind.

Normally, a life map includes certain landmark events, life-cycle transitions. These can be based on biology, such as puberty, or can be given by culture, such as college graduation. But the life map need not be restricted to these. It is a narrative I construct, a narrative whose structure I will examine in much greater detail in the next chapters. Like the worldview, it is not meant to block out experience but to make ordered experiencing possible. Moreover, it is even more adaptable than the worldview, a portrait open and vulnerable to many kinds of revisions.

But it is not infinitely adaptable and changeable. There are certain biological givens and certain cultural conditions that function as givens. For example, in no human culture can biological motherhood begin at age sixty, nor can a ten-year-old child perform open-heart surgery. No viable life maps can find room for such options. Moreover, the categories I require for my life map must be limited to those that are culturally available or those I create myself out of ingredients that are available. How plausible my life map is depends on my social setting, so that it matters if I live in a culture without official puberty rites for women but with high school and college graduation ceremonies. Even if I deliberately remap my life by borrowing categories from a culture and tradition not my own (if I start to understand who I am in terms of previous incarnations and the law of fate, for example), I will probably be unable to escape the influence of my own North American perspective in doing so.

With that caution in mind, we can examine how this definition of religion as worldview and life map relates to the more conventional sense of what religion is. One view is that the convention (religion in the sense of consciously held beliefs, etc.) is simply a by-product of *real* religion as found in the worldview. Thomas Luckmann writes of an American worldview that constitutes an "invisible religion"; it may well be true that much of American Christianity and Judaism is best understood as an expression of this invisible, unconsciously held worldview. On the other hand, this same approach can lead to absurd conclusions. The sixteenth-century mystic Teresa of Avila held a worldview distinctively Spanish, which today even the average reader of her writings can sense. But it would be extremely odd to say that she was therefore not so much Catholic as Spanish! Her Spanishness shaped her Christianity, but one was not a side effect or by-product of the other.

Another approach claims there exists some "Christian" worldview that can be isolated and contrasted to the worldviews, for example, of contemporary North America or sixteenth-century Spain. This line of argument has been popular in times past and continues to be advocated by some today. There is, they claim, a distinctively Christian vision of reality, a system of symbols, moods, motivations, and the like. This Christian worldview was transmitted by the ancient Hebrews and the mostly Hellenized Jews of the New Testament church; it remains an eternal norm that must be held while all alternative worldviews must be rejected.

But of what exactly does this Christian worldview consist? Here, the variety of answers is striking. For Augustine, say, writing in late antiquity, a metaphysical theory based on the thought of Plato is a kind of prerequisite for faith in Christ. To hear the gospel properly requires that we hold a certain philosophical vision of reality in which spirit and matter, eternity and time, are sharply divided. One must, then, be at least an informal Platonist in order to make sense of scripture.[6] This yielded a mazeway that was philosophically rigorous and coherent and thus acceptable to an intellectual such as Augustine. It was internally consistent; it fit together as a system and could be taught as one. In contrast, some Protestant thinkers in the twentieth century have gone in an opposite direction, drawing a hard line between Augustine's Greek worldview and the Hebraic one, which is for them the *real* Christian worldview.[7] Their idea seems to be, like Augustine's, that such a worldview is the only one that truly fits the core of Christian faith.

But from these examples, I can draw a rather different conclusion: Christianity has apparently survived massive shifts in worldview—and has done so in spite of claims that it requires a particular worldview to convey its meanings. Major religious traditions do seem to outlive a variety of supposedly necessary worldviews, and their travel from culture to culture is possible precisely because they are flexible. The transition from one worldview to another includes some pain and strain, but it is a possibility. This is why there can be Christians in Korea or in Africa today, where presumably the cultural and philosophical prerequisites cannot be those Augustine saw as necessary. Christianity may not be compatible with *any* worldview, but it has spanned a good many of them. Whatever all Christians everywhere and at all times share, it is *not* a worldview in the sense given that term by theorists of religion.

Yet the biblical texts and their images (upon which all forms of Christianity rest) come from communities of persons whose worldviews are those of past cultures. Paul, the Fourth Evangelist, and Jesus of Nazareth himself all lived as first-century persons, in societies holding visions of the world very different from mine or from any I would want to hold. In this sense, they are forever distant from me; to be incarnate means to be fully part of some time, place, and culture—and this particular time, place, and culture is not mine. The same thing holds true for other texts and their authors, of course. Shakespeare's plays, with their ghosts and portents and Elizabethan views of kingship, are an excellent example.

But—as this second example especially may help me realize—so what if worldviews differ? I cannot hear Shakespeare as did the patrons of the original Globe Theatre, and I cannot appreciate Paul's baptismal symbolism as did the first readers of the Letter to the Romans. But hearing and appreciating in this way are never what we mean when we say we understand Romans or enjoy Shakespeare's plays. In fact, most of us can rightly claim some major advantages over the audiences of the Globe: We have the entire corpus of plays, several centuries of Shakespeare criticism, and a long tradition of acting and stagecraft to draw upon in performing. And similarly, to "understand" the New Testament is not to become an honorary first-century person (whatever that would mean) but to allow the words of the New Testament to be heard by us—twentieth-century persons indebted to Augustine, Luther, and the many others who have pondered Paul's texts. Worldviews are not enclosed, self-contained, and impervious to correction. We can indeed receive messages from those whose vision of reality was substantially different from ours. There are differences in worldview, obviously, but these are simply not solid obstacles blocking off all thought and life from another era or culture. Unfortunately, some who have pondered this problem have considered them as such.

But what then is the relation between worldview—mine or that of the first-century Christians—and the ultimate contents of Christian faith? A third approach is the well-known demythologizing project of Rudolf Bultmann. Working as both a biblical scholar and a theologian, Bultmann tried to separate "kerygma" —the fundamental proclamation of the Gospel—from "myth,"[8] or, in our terms, the first-century worldview presupposed by the authors of the New Testament. The worldview of the New Testament writers assumed a three-level universe inhabited by angels and demons, an apocalyptic view of history, and a God ever ready to perform miraculous acts such as exorcisms and resurrections—all of which Bultmann labeled "prescientific" and no longer credible for us today. But the kerygma, the true core of what Christian faith is *really* about, depends upon none of these beliefs. The specific solution Bultmann proposed was that kerygma could be expressed for twentieth-century persons ("modern man") using the alternative worldview framework provided by Martin Heidegger's existentialist philosophy.[9]

In at least one way, this project of Bultmann's can serve as a model for our present task. If worldview and core Christian realities can be separated, we need not make any specific philosophy or *ism* a necessary prerequisite for holding to faith in Christ. This means that I am free to use contemporary psychology, for example, to help reveal what Bultmann called "the kerygma," without fear that I will automatically betray the latter. I can also recognize that psychology (like Heidegger's existentialism!) fits within my worldview but is alien to that of first-century Hellenistic culture.

However, the specific terms used by Bultmann confuse the general problem of faith and worldviews with the more specific issue of myth and science. Here I find Bultmann quite unhelpful and far too much of a rationalist to serve as a guide for how to read the Bible as a modern person. Ironically, even Heidegger uses myth and poetry to philosophize! Surely the continuing need of twentieth-century persons for imagery, metaphor, and symbol ought to give us more respect for the imagery of the New Testament authors than Bultmann had. As I will insist, even the cosmological imagery of the New Testament, its vision of earth and heaven and the underworld, can be potentially reinvested with meaning, although not for use by geologists. Most centrally, the term "kerygma" depersonalizes the way the core Christian reality is apprehended. Christ, and not primarily a proclamation about Christ or a faith state engendered by this proclamation, is what—*who*—really counts, for the Christian.

Suppose, therefore, that, instead of a core kerygma which stands outside particular worldviews, we substitute the living God known in and through Christ. Through the central events of creation, redemption, and consummation, through Jesus' cross and resurrection and return, this God is known. These "events" (and I am aware that Bultmann for one would not consider all of them events in the usual sense at all) are landmarks in a spiritual geography, a landscape never directly apprehended save through the mazeways and worldviews and life maps we possess. What all Christians everywhere and at all times share is the encounter with the events of this landscape, through which the living God in Jesus Christ is encountered. This meeting drastically affects our cultural mazeways and individual life maps, forcing their revision in numerous ways. But because the mazeways are themselves so different, the particular revisions will also be different.

Spiritual geography should not necessarily be construed as a sublime territory lying above the ordinary realm of physical geography (as in the vertical map to be discussed in chapter 6). Yet the term is intended to imply a range of reality and experience unknown apart from the encounter with the living God known in Jesus Christ. In light of this encounter, even the familiar mapped and mazewayed world looks very different. Spiritual geography is not only a different territory, it permits me to see the previously known territory more truly and in proper proportion. For some, this image of spiritual geography may feel too spatial, too static, especially for a faith that has so often been described as valuing time above space, "holy history" above "holy places." However, the function of this term is to help us examine various models of life maps and show how they construct experience in time. We will be thoroughly engaged in the problems of time, of how individuals order their pasts, presents, and futures. Because of the spatial metaphor given in terms such as mazeway, an equally spatial construct of geography seems called for.

Baptism is my entrance into this spiritual geography, as a rite of initiation. And more important to us, its imagery links the central landmarks of spiritual geography to my life. Baptismal imagery is, then, a kind of gate into spiritual geography, a beginning place that will have impact upon the various models of life map I may hold. In the chapters that follow, some basic models of life maps will be described and their possible relations with the fundamental baptismal imagery explored.

4
Three Patterns
of Life Maps

A life map is meant for me as a guide to reality—the realities of the social and physical world—and to my own inner reality as it unfolds within the larger, culturally shaped context. A life map, like a worldview, need not be consciously held or clearly articulated for it to work well for the person who uses it. Life maps are intended primarily to help me guide myself through the mysteries and pitfalls of existence. They do not have to lay out a full systematic theology or philosophy. What a life map must do is make reality and individual destiny meaningful for me. It need not make my life easy in the sense of problem-free. It will, if it works at all, give me a sense that I am engaged in living a life that holds together, one that I can survey as a coherent unity rather than merely as a hodgepodge of unrelated experiences.

In chapter 3 we saw that the living God and Christian spiritual geography may be apprehended through a variety of diverse worldviews. There is no one "Christian" worldview. This same position holds true for life maps, the individualized editions of worldviews. There is no need to search for or create one and only one Christian pattern of life map, to be shared by all Christians everywhere. There may be value in having an explicit, articulated form of life map rather than a tacit, taken-for-granted one. But this should not be mistaken for the claim that only one sort of life map is built into the Christian faith, to serve as an ideal and a standard for everyone.

Nevertheless, it makes sense to ask, What kind of life maps have Christians relied on? A thorough answer to this question might demand a historical survey of the variety of patterns available in different branches of Christianity at different times. For our purpose, a typology is more helpful, to sort the many specific examples of life maps into a small number of basic patterns. I believe that there exist at least three distinguishable styles of life map drawn by Christians. These three maps are not by now unique to Christians, for, once created, they have continued to influence other map makers. Psychologists working in a post-Christendom cultural context have perpetuated all three models, as we shall see.

Are these three maps unique to Christianity? Do they depend upon its own specific spiritual geography for their very existence? If post-Christian psychology can use these same styles of map, could Buddhists or Native Americans share them too? Cross-cultural studies of biography and autobiography provide ambivalent answers to this question.[1] When a life map is linked to a cosmology—a total picture of the physical-spiritual universe —the answer is, Yes, there are parallels and similarities between Christian and non-Christian cosmologies. It is clear that the mystical ladders of Christian contemplative spirituality parallel the many-leveled models of inward experience of ultimate reality found in Buddhism and other traditions. Another pattern, closer to autobiography as a literary genre, appears to depend upon either Christianity or the classical Greco-Roman heritage of the West, or both. This is not found among Buddhists or Jews or in many other religious traditions.

What is certain, however, is that there is no necessary historical progress from simpler to more complex types of life map. The model I see as the most complex is usually ascribed to Augustine, the supreme autobiographer. Augustine, according to James Olney, writes "the double sort of autobiography"—he is aware that he is not merely retelling the adventures of a self but is engaged in becoming one through his autobiographical activity.[2] And the best example of the simplest model comes from a far later historical period than that of Augustine. Instances of both can be found today, alive and well, in contemporary psychological theory. In fact, speaking of the forms of autobiography, William Spengemann states, "Although not everything done today has always been done, it is probably fair to say that everything that has ever been done is still being done, somewhere."[3] When we see how models of Christian life maps have been developed within psychology, this is certainly true.

This statement, however, raises the question of whether all life maps count as autobiography in the literary sense. If not, what is the relation between autobiography as a genre of literature and what I am calling "life map"? This is no easy question to answer, especially because the question "What makes a written work an autobiography?" is itself now hotly debated. It is not clear that the best examples of autobiography always *look* like autobiographies. We naively assume that an autobiography should straightforwardly tell the story of an individual's life, with that same person as narrator and protagonist. But even Augustine himself does not fit this picture, for the final four books of *Confessions* are not, strictly speaking, autobiography in the conventional sense. In them, Augustine meditates on memory and time and ties his personal story to the great story of God's creation of the world. And if this is how Augustine thought, contemporary definitions of autobiography can become even further removed from our naive definition. For example, the two theorists cited already, Olney and Spengemann, include chapters on Eliot's "Four Quartets" and Hawthorne's *The Scarlet Letter* in works devoted to autobiography! Hence, my own typology of life-map models will include some obviously autobiographical forms but, also, other works. Some of these may meet a literary theorist's nontraditional criteria for autobiography. Nevertheless, this is not why they will be important for us.

The Horizontal Pattern

The most straightforward of the three life-map patterns or models is one I will call horizontal. Its spatial imagery perceives human existence as a journey from a point A to a point B, a journey filled with adventures and dangers but a journey very like ordinary travel in physical geography. There are a number of specially marked places in this journey that every traveler can expect to pass and which should surprise no one. The journey is easily mappable, visualized as a progression from here to there. Once mapped, the landscape becomes more manageable, and each individual can feel competent to negotiate its hazards.

The favorite instance of this model in Christian spiritual literature is John Bunyan's *The Pilgrim's Progress*. Bunyan's book depends, naturally enough, upon an idea of pilgrimage that flowered during medieval times as an actual religious ritual. To go on a pilgrimage meant to take a journey in physical geography toward some goal with meaning in spiritual geography as well. Jerusalem, Rome, many national and local shrines: all served as sacred centers, and by traveling to such places the pilgrim could approach the Holy, the place on earth where God was especially present. This ancient pattern continued to flourish in spite of the tremendous dangers of travel. But by the late Middle Ages, it had become interiorized. One could use a devotional guidebook and conduct an imaginative pilgrimage in one's own home. This eliminated the physical journey (and its expenses) but was intended to preserve—and, indeed, to augment—the basic spiritual intention of the trip. The Reformation rejected pilgrimage as a spiritual activity but kept the theme of life as a pilgrimage without much tension. Interestingly, one feature of real pilgrimage in physical geography got lost in this spiritualization: the return trip, the way back from the sacred center to one's starting point. Horizontal life maps eliminate this feature entirely.

A journey from point A to point B: This is the essence of a horizontal map. For Bunyan, these were not to be equated with birth and death, because his life map was meant for religious, not biological, existence. The starting place was also not baptism, which plays no role in the landscape of *Pilgrim's Progress.* Instead, it is conversion, the moment on the very first page when the man with the book in his hand and the burden on his back cries, "What shall I do to be saved?"[4] The man—whose existence before this time holds no interest to Bunyan or the reader— learns that his point A is the City of Destruction, from which he must flee. His goal, point B, is the Celestial City. His progress is mapped out by the author from this starting place until his final triumphant arrival at his goal.

Bunyan is writing a religious life map, not a biological one. Events that most of us would consider intrinsic to the life cycle, and nearly universal, are given no attention, or very minimal attention. Christian, the hero of Part I, is married and has a family. But when he fails to persuade them to leave the City of Destruction with him, he runs off, covering his ears to deafen himself to their pleas begging him to remain.[5] Henceforth, although his life is made up of continuous meetings and adventures, none of these connect back to his family life. The sole life-cycle event that does interest Bunyan is death, but not because it is a biological given. Death is one peril of the soul among many for Christian and his companions. They must cross a river to arrive at the Celestial City, and it is this spiritual transition that interests Bunyan. Moreover, to cross the river does not mean safe arrival; death is no guarantee of salvation. "There was a way to hell even from the gates of heaven, as well as from the City of Destruction."[6]

Bunyan's allegory was intended to be explicit; the reader is never meant to be left in doubt as to what is being symbolized. Certainly, the names of characters—Mr. Money-love, Mr. Worldly Wiseman—are meant to be obvious, requiring no additional interpretation. Bunyan's style of Protestantism did not make use of spiritual directors or what Protestants today would call "discipleship training." But *Pilgrim's Progress* was intended to serve a function similar to that of a spiritual director. Every adventure in the allegory represents something likely to happen to many if not to all Christians as they travel through this land of darkness and evil toward the bright lights of the Celestial City.

For example, Christian must pass through a terrible Valley of Humiliation, where he encounters a demonic opponent named Apollyon. This monster challenges him, declaring, "Thou art one of my subjects." He berates Christian for deserting his service and reminds the poor terrified traveler of his failures during his pilgrimage. Christian admits to these (in the Valley of Humiliation) but stands fast. "Then Apollyon straddled quite over the whole breadth of the way, and said, I am void of fear in this matter. Prepare thyself to die." A hideous battle ensues, with Christian the victor in spite of being sorely wounded.[7]

Can this scene be de-allegorized? Yes, insofar as Bunyan ties the facing of an absolute evil to the experience of humiliation and to the fear that in spite of all movement one remains unchanged, a hopeless sinner once and always. To put this thought in the mouth of the demon reveals it as a lie, and a lie to be struggled against with all one's might. The monster threatens death, but—as a Christian must recognize—the sure spiritual death is to flee in fright and return to what one was before. Whether a creature like Apollyon really exists or not is beside the point; the lie he represents is monstrous, faithless and deadly at some very basic level.

Readers of Louisa M. Alcott's *Little Women* may recognize how an episode like this could be part of using Bunyan as a life map. The young heroines "play pilgrims" in meeting conflicts and obstacles in their lives, guided by their wise mother. "Jo Meets Apollyon" when she lets her anger at her younger sister blind her to Amy's danger when they go ice-skating. The spirit of evil, vengeful anger, temporarily controls her. Later, in great shame, she takes the blame for Amy's falling through the ice and expresses despair over ever mastering her bad temper. The mother listens and confesses that her own outward calm is the product of long years of intense self-mastery over anger. "Apollyon" is both the vicious anger itself and the lie that it can never be conquered.[8] Here, Bunyan's allegory is directly appropriated; presumably, what the March family did in fiction, others did (albeit less self-consciously) in fact.

Today, this use of *Pilgrim's Progress* is extremely difficult, even among the most devout. Readers today are much more likely to enjoy the book's charm, its lively blend of traditional fairy-tale motifs (monsters, castles, and giants) with energetic dialogues. Like many fairy tales, the work proceeds from point A to point B through a series of seemingly disconnected incidents, adventures in the form of tests for the hero. But to use this work as a life map requires that we perceive the goal of Christian life to be arrival at the Celestial City, with this life a journey to be traversed as quickly as possible. Homecoming, light, and safety lie farther ahead, while the work we experience in this life is on the whole dismal, dark, and dangerous. Although Bunyan never confused being saved with being dead, the model of a linear progression makes salvation something available only at the end.

Horizontal life maps are, by definition, flat. The end is construed as point B, not as another dimension of the entire landscape. Thus, to call Bunyan's allegory "otherworldly" is confusing. The Celestial City becomes a place in horizontal space on the same plane as the City of Destruction. Perhaps Bunyan's model is not otherworldly enough, for it is limited to the earth's surface as the space where travel is possible. Yet in an ingenious scene, his hero in the midst of his journey is permitted to gaze through a telescope at his goal, the towers of the Celestial City. They shine far away, too bright to behold amid the darkness of this world.[9] This brief vision stretches to its limit the basic structure of the horizontal model.

The Vertical Pattern

A vertical life map resolves this problem. In such a model, human existence is depicted as located in the midst of a multi-level cosmos, a geography within which up and down are the main directions and the chief options for movement. A vertical map may indeed be used as what I have termed an individual life map, but it also seems to be dependent on a cosmology, a map of the physical and spiritual universe held by an entire culture or community. If *The Pilgrim's Progress* is the best-known example for a horizontal map, Dante's *Divine Comedy* provides our clearest instance of a vertical life map. Dante's setting is in fact the official cosmos of his entire culture, of medieval Christianity. Moreover, the vision of the universe as layered, a finite series of spheres, is not unique to Dante's era or to Christianity at all. Parallels to this model can be found within most of the classic religious traditions, in the form of various mystical ladders East and West. A vertical map thus includes a belief in what Rudolf Bultmann derided as "the three-storied universe" of biblical cosmology.[10] It requires a "below" and an "above," from which events upon earth's surface can be seen in new perspective, and earth's surface itself is made relative as one realm of several.

Dante's vertical map portrays a universe held whole, and which includes absolutely everything and everyone known or knowable. The eternal realms of the Hell, Purgatory, and Paradise through which the poet moves provide a cosmic grid, within which exist every kind of person and supernatural being. The poet and his guides, Virgil and Beatrice, meet persons from the Bible (St. John, Adam), from classical mythology (Ulysses), and from contemporary Italy; they also encounter demons, the Gorgon, angelic beings of various sorts, and allegorical rivers, trees, and the like. From the different places within this cosmos, the reader receives new perspectives on the earth's surface, especially on the author's wretched city of Florence. For today's reader, of course, the work must be read with a double grid—both the cosmic order and the historical setting of the struggles between pope and emperor, the warring factions of Guelphs and Ghibellines—neither one overly familiar to most of us. Yet Dante's cosmos, however large-scale and inclusive when contrasted to Bunyan's, is overwhelmingly knowable and ordered.

The order, as with most vertical maps, is a hierarchy, a set of levels: the lower that one descends, the more evil; the higher, the more pure. Everyone has his or her place in this order. Those at the lowest level of Paradise—blessed but inferior in status to those closer to God—are asked if they wish to be higher up. They reply that such an elevation would violate divine justice and thus bring them pain.[11] So the ladder works as a kind of divinely ordered rating scale; from the placement of a certain group of damned or blessed souls, one knows the relative value of the quality that was their outstanding attribute. In general, sins of the flesh are less evil than sins of violence or betrayal, so those who committed them are placed higher in the Inferno—and in Purgatory as well. It is worse to be proud than to be a glutton, and worse to betray one's country than to steal.

However, the cosmic grid is, in fact, ordered by categories provided by Aristotle and medieval moral philosophy based on his thought. This results in classifications and ratings that do not correspond at all to our values. For example, Dante and his guide Virgil progress downward through hell into the wood of the suicides, "the violent against themselves." Dante is deeply moved by these souls, locked in trees, who can speak only when their leaves are torn and bleed (a striking image of suicide's meaning). He next meets "the violent against nature." Today this phrase might refer to polluters of the environment, but Dante uses it to mean sodomites, those whose sexuality denied the natural good of procreation. They run across a sandy, fiery plain epitomizing the sterility of their sin. The next level downward is for "the violent against art," the usurers who lent money for interest. Their sin was defined according to a medieval definition of money as "infertile"—making interest earned on money its "unnatural" offspring. For usurers, Dante has little but contempt and hatred. However odd this progression from suicides to homosexuals to loan sharks seems to us, ironically the poet's own sympathies seem to follow very contemporary lines.[12]

A correlate of this vertical rating is that persons of equal value appear together, regardless of distance in history or any other factors that separated them in life. Figures from classical epics and mythology exist side by side in the Inferno with Dante's fellow Florentines, united only in sharing the same category of sin. At the other end of the scale, Dominic and Francis belong together in the fourth sphere of Paradise, among the Doctors of the Church, although the orders they founded were in bitter rivalry during Dante's era.

Dante's map is ahistorical, as are all vertical maps. For its principal inhabitants are all eternal, all outside the flow of time as we experience it on earth's surface. The dead are fixed in their existence, their fate; even the souls in Purgatory, who live in anticipation of entry into Paradise proper, are in some sense already there and no longer in suspense as to their eternal status. The Last Judgment will consummate what is already a known and fixed order of reality. And so, in this map death itself takes on a different meaning from that in Bunyan's, where it came at the end of life's long and difficult journey. Death is above and beneath, a condition of timelessness in which each soul's true inner essence is revealed. To know reality is to visit the three realms of the dead, to know all the options of sin and blessedness, and to recognize them within oneself by meeting them in others. But above the realm of the human dead is the final and highest sphere of Paradise, where the Godhead dwells. This, the Eternal Good, encompasses the entire order:

> I saw within Its depth how It conceives
> all things in a single volume bound by Love,
> of which the universe is the scattered leaves.[13]

Because a journey can only be construed in time, the poet's trip takes time to tell, and he and we can grasp the total landscape only serially. But the eternality of the order is still the ultimate reality, for God knows it all as simultaneously present, a volume bound together and read by him all at once, in its totality. No need in this map for a return journey, for a descent back to earth's surface. The goal is accomplished with the beatific vision, for the Eternal Good encompasses and transcends everything that can be experienced, everything that has gone before or can come later.

As we shall see, vertical maps are enjoying a limited renaissance today within the field of psychology. But for most of us they pose certain problems, even more than do horizontal maps. The cosmology that once made them literally real is now gone. The moral grid that Dante could assume, the one-dimensional rating system, no longer makes sense to us as a way to identify degrees and kinds of evil or good. Suicide and loan-sharking are both evils, but their relation to each other cannot be expressed using Dante's moral system. Today's debates over homosexuality do not ask if it is better or worse than usury or suicide, although the often-used adjective "unnatural" retains some of Dante's echoes. A third problem is that the very idea of an eternal realm, or of realms outside history, appears impossible to those for whom history and change are everything. How can one allow for growth and change in a universe as ordered, as complete, as bounded as Dante's? Is there not something wholly static about such a life map? I believe that a vertical life map does allow for growth of a sort, but it is growth within an order that sets limits as well as provides possibilities. It is fair to call a map such as Dante's, in which the realms above and beneath the earth's surface are clearly realms of the afterlife, "otherworldly" even more thoroughly than Bunyan's. The whole point of any vertical map is, as I said before, to relativize the claims and perspectives of earth's surface by showing earth to be one of many possible places, and not necessarily the most real or eternal of these. This is a goal problematic and threatening to many.

The Spiral Pattern

Both horizontal and vertical maps are relatively simple in structure and easy to describe. They complement each other. The third model for mapping individual existence is less simple and less easy to recognize. It is not by any means the creation of the twentieth century, yet some of the best examples are to be found in our era.

The key idea behind this model is that a lived existence proceeds in loops; it reaches forward toward the future, partly by a return motion which establishes a new relation with the past. The return, the loop of the spiral, includes as much discovery as the thrust forward. The past is not left behind, as in the horizontal map, but is seen and regained afresh whenever a new loop is completed. To express this, a three-dimensional spiral is required. For the return to the past is a reflective reengagement with earlier life, mediated through memory; it is not a literal backtracking from point B to point A. The very act of reflective return re-creates point A, so that the past reseen and reapprehended is never identical to the past when first lived.

Spiral maps are used by sophisticated autobiographers, of whom Augustine in his *Confessions* remains the best example. *Confessions* is an extended prayer addressed to God, the Source of Augustine's being, the hidden agent in his troubled life, and the true goal of his desiring. God already knows the narrator protagonist better than Augustine knows himself, but the process of confessing, telling his story to God (and to the reader), invites self-knowledge. The past Augustine remembers is, overwhelmingly, a *sinful* past. In a key incident, he recalls an act of vandalism done for sheer perversity; he and his companions threw away the pears they had stolen.[14] Sin is pointless, but it is pervasive and endemic to the human condition. The conflict deepens, as Augustine's intellectual questionings become mingled with his personal torments:

> I was unhappy, and so is every soul unhappy which is tied to its love for mortal things; when it loses them, it is torn in pieces, and it is then that it comes to realize the unhappiness which was there even before it lost them.[15]

From Augustine's Christian standpoint, in reviewing his own sinful past he can now recognize how God was at work through his unhappiness—drawing the sinful soul to himself. The climax of the narrative is the fulfillment of this process: Augustine's conversion, where, as for Saul and Cyprian, the old self and its doubts die. The protagonist can become Augustine the Christian, author of the *Confessions,* who can see his own story as one of the mighty works of God. Incidentally, it also becomes edifying for others—or else he never would have circulated this work.

But Augustine recognizes that he is not merely tracing the progress of an already finished self from point A to point B. Wise authors of this sort of spiral autobiography hope to recover not only lost time but a lost or unknown self. In the very process of his or her work, the author brings a self into being who did not exist before the writing. The spiral map maker holds that the past cannot be left behind—and, indeed, should not be. Yet the past as ordinarily remembered is not the truest past but a kind of screen, which prevents a deeper access to what the past might really mean, what it might really have to say to the self who

searches for it. Augustine's unhappy past is truly the past where
God was elusively present. It is this message that provides the
impetus for the thrust forward, the sense of a loop rather than
merely a return. In the words of James Olney:

> Emotion, experience, life—whatever name we give it—is merely
> a subjective fact for us at loose ends, a formless and chaotic and
> painful mass, until we are far enough removed to see the total
> pattern, from beginning to necessary end, and, if it be a circle, as
> so many poets and mystics would have it, to new beginning. Then,
> in the recapture of the experience as a formal, patterned whole,
> we realize at last the meaning, and perception of meaning is the
> greatest satisfaction, the richest reward.[16]

Within an autobiography, this process takes the form of narrat-
ing how the "I" came into being, the one and only "I" who
could ever tell this particular story. Current theories of autobiography are not interested in whether the story is historically accurate.[17] Was Augustine at age twenty really so wretched as the
forty-five-year-old narrator makes him out to have been? The
question is irrelevant as well as historically unanswerable. These
theorists favor a theory of autobiographical truth based on poetic
unity. Every autobiographer reconstructs and re-creates both the
past and the self, often at the expense of historical details. The
aware autobiographer is the one who self-consciously recognizes
this process. Yet an autobiography can, sadly, lie. This occurs
when the experiences fail to become a formal patterned whole,
in spite of the narrator's strident insistence that they form one.
Another type of lie exists when the protagonist whose adventures fill the narrative is simply not the same person as the narrator, regardless of the fact that they share the same name. A
narrator who like Augustine stresses the sinful nature of his own
past, but who in unguarded moments emerges from the pages as
an optimistic, happy-go-lucky character, will be unbelievable.
These autobiographical lies are harder to identify than factual
inaccuracies—but at some point we disbelieve the entire book,
the author's whole project.

Traditional autobiography is, however, not the only literary
genre to depend on a spiral model for its vitality. Although it
may seem odd to group *Confessions* with works of entertainment,
detective stories also require this complex loop of a reflective

return to the past. A detective story typically begins with the crime and ends when the detective has been able to reconstruct what really happened, the events in the past that led up to it. When the events—however complicated, improbable, and bizarre—can be told in proper sequence, the story is over. The mystery is not just whodunit but what the past really was like—in contrast to what the readers and most of the characters believe it to have been. As we shall see, Freudian case histories follow this pattern, with the analyst as sleuth.

But even a detective is superfluous, if the murderer can provide a detailed account of how the confusing and mysterious jumble of events was actually a perfectly logical sequence of meaningful actions. An example would be Agatha Christie's *And Then There Were None,* where the judge responsible for all the deaths reveals the entire sequence to the final victim, whom he has driven to the brink of suicide. Here, as with Augustine, the format of confession bridges the gulf between protagonist and narrator.

We cannot even begin to imagine the plots of most classic detective fiction reorganized to fit a horizontal linear format, beginning from point A and progressing through point B. It is the past, not the future, that is unknown and requires disclosure, as when the tortured, long-concealed relations between murderer and victim are made known. A spiral map requires a complex vision of the past as well as an awareness that the past never dies, never becomes obliterated or disappears. It may lose some of its power through re-visioning, through the reflective return of the spiral's loop, but this loss is replaced by a new understanding of the whole, of the circle from which the self receives meaning.

To illustrate the difference between this map and the horizontal, we may take for an example a work that tries to combine both —and partially fails, as a result. This work is C. S. Lewis's *The Pilgrim's Regress,* a book that even the most devoted Lewis fans will find rough going. Lewis wanted to write an account of how he became a Christian—a spiritual autobiography, emphasizing his intellectual journey through philosophical idealism and Romanticism. He could have used—and later did use—the conventional autobiographical form, the style set for conversion narratives by Augustine. (This work, *Surprised by Joy,* is far more readable than *Regress.*) Instead, Lewis turned to allegory, relying explicitly on Bunyan for his format.

The plot begins at point A, the land of Puritania where his hero, John, is born and grows to adolescence. While in a nearby wood, he spies a lovely island, very far off. He leaves home to find the island and wanders through a landscape meant to portray the intellectual and moral climate of early twentieth-century Europe. The hero finally converts to Christianity; in the imagery of the allegory, he crosses a chasm with the help of Mother Kirk, in an explicitly baptismal initiation.[18] There he sees up close the beautiful island he had first gazed on long ago as an adolescent. He then begins a return journey—a "regress"—back across the same landscape he crossed before. This time, however, it is seen as it really is: a dismal, dangerous swamp, filled with miserable and repulsive temptations and dangers which are now obvious rather than hidden. The book ends, as Bunyan's does, with the hero's death, as he crosses a river out of the territory of this world. He enters the mountains of the Landlord who rules the earth, mountains which are none other than his beloved island from the other side, properly known.

Although there are many flaws to the book, its most interesting one is that it confounds two separate models of a life map. Lewis is interested in the past, in retracing his steps and seeing even his most lawless and lost experiences as, in some sense, part of his progress toward God. Like Augustine, then, he must see his past anew in the light of his present. He wants to show that his life and his intellectual development portray a formal, patterned whole and are not just the disconnected series of trials and errors they must have seemed at the time. Given this task, the portrayal of the places visited is Lewis's Christian portrait of them. The flaws he sees are the flaws as revealed to him *now,* at the time he writes, not at the time he himself stumbled into such countries, which he now names Claptrap and Zeitgeistheim ("home of the spirit of the times").[19] To label them thus is already the privilege of the autobiographer's superior knowledge, his capacity to see the folly and futility of the past for what it was. But if so, then the "regress" through the landscape adds virtually nothing; Lewis has already given us an appraisal of the places where he lingered along the way. Moreover, all the adventures that Bunyan placed in the path of his hero are assigned by Lewis to the preconversion journey. The real issue is not "Will the hero make it to the Heavenly City?" but "How and when will he make it across the chasm (conversion)?" Nothing much is left to experience postconversion, except the intense awareness of the world as a dreary and disgusting place. No Christian writer wants to give the impression that existence postconversion is drearier and more boring than it was before!

Bunyan and Augustine are effective taken individually, but not when conflated in this way. The emotional tone of distaste and moral harshness for which Lewis later apologized[20] arises in large part from this unsatisfactory conjunction. Lewis's book is worth this attention because it shows how even an imaginative and skillful writer can get trapped in the conflicting limitations of various life maps. As a recent convert, Lewis wanted to make his journey public. But even a more ordinary adult convert must do—implicitly, if not explicitly—some of what *The Pilgrim's Regress* sets out to do. Converts need not write a literary autobiography or a defense of their conversion. But they must confront the issue of a beginning place, or a re-visioned life map. The imagery of baptism, of death to the sinful self, and of new birth requires such a re-visioning and remapping.

5
The Horizontal Life Map and the Myth of the Fresh Start

What happens when baptismal imagery of death-resurrection with Christ and new birth is integrated into a horizontal style of life map? Within such a framework, baptism's function as beginning place for entrance into spiritual geography becomes concentrated upon the overwhelming sense of *newness* that sparkles from the biblical imagery. "You have died" and now live to God. A Christian is a "new creation." "The old has passed away, behold, the new has come." The life now lived is a walk in newness, discontinuous with whatever went before. "Birth" is even more decisive and dramatic. When I am born from water and the Spirit, I am an entirely new being, essentially unconnected to the person born from woman sometime in the past.

There are two clear consequences of this imagery of newness. One is to provide hope, hope that change is possible and that God will be both willing and able to bring it about. Faith in Christ offers a way to bring men and women out of death and into life, out of enslavement to "the rulers of this age" and into a life of reconciliation and redemption. God acting in Christ had made this possible and helps each baptized person live out this transformation in every area of his or her existence.

The second direct consequence of this language is to turn persons against their own pasts, now construed as times of darkness and evil. This style of emphasis upon newness raises the expectation that the entire past can vanish, being buried in Christ's tomb—to die, never to rise up again. And by implication, because this language of death-resurrection and new birth is sufficiently drastic, it seems to idealize an image of an entirely past-less person. For such a person, a complete fresh start is not only possible but required.

Let me define as the myth of the fresh start this belief that the past can be obliterated, killed off so definitely that it need never be brought to mind, nor will it ever continue to act as an influence in the individual's ongoing existence. The term "myth" is used here to mean not a necessarily false belief but a powerful, primordial motif of human yearning and possibility. Before I can answer the question "Is this kind of newness what Paul and the other New Testament authors intended by their baptismal imagery?" I must see the myth of the fresh start as a powerful force in my own North American twentieth-century worldview.

The appeal and power of this myth becomes clear when I see its connection with the horizontal model of a life map as described in the previous chapter. The horizontal model sees individual existence as a journey from point A to point B, a journey through time marked by departures. Although John Bunyan's *Pilgrim's Progress* provides the chief example of this model, there are many others. These horizontal life maps are distinguished by a certain optimism about the possibility of departure. Bunyan's hero, Christian, leaves the City of Destruction, never again to return. The various adventures in his path toward the Celestial City test and mature him but are not intrinsically connected by Bunyan to Christian's earlier life. Once one says good-bye to it, the past can be truly left behind. This optimism about departure pervades editions of the horizontal life map where no connection with Christianity is maintained. The map itself requires it.

There is one such secularized version of this pattern that plays a particularly important role for those of us in North American society. Since colonial times, the American people have traditionally endorsed just this style of life map, envisioning our country as the land of the fresh start. North America is the continent settled by persons who traveled from some point A far away to begin life again in the New World. Emigration and western expansion together endorsed this pattern. Geographical mobility meant that one could literally leave one's past behind and continue one's life journey somewhere else. This country, to a degree hard to overestimate, was settled by families and individuals who did obliterate their own pasts, their own previous habits and cultural patterns. In spite of the fact that ethnicity remains a reality of American life, the ideal of America as a melting pot existed as a powerful expression of the myth of the fresh start.[1] The old customs, languages, costumes "died," were abandoned in the crucible of the melting pot; what emerged was a new person, an American, an individual without a past but with a wide-open present and immense expectations for the future.

We may wonder if the melting pot is not indirectly derived from Christian sources. Is it an image of absolute newness, created by a nation that once considered itself the New Israel, liberated from slavery in the Old World? Perhaps. But the reverse question is far more relevant: Does the still-powerful image of the American melting pot influence the way I read the New Testament imagery of baptismal newness? If so, does this influence clarify or obscure the biblical hope for "newness of life?" As an American, I am soaked from my natural birth in the culture that produced and in some fashion still believes in the ideal of the melting pot. If I intend to appropriate Christian images of newness, will I not risk confusing the two? This is an excellent instance of worldview interfacing with spiritual geography, exactly the kind of problem addressed in chapter 3. Like Teresa of Avila's Spanishness, my participation in American society and its worldview may permeate my apprehension of certain key themes from Christianity.

But that there *is* some similarity is hard to deny. Just as a variety of immigrant groups were melted into one new being, the American, so baptism can overcome such divisions as Jew and Greek, slave and free, male and female (Gal. 3:28). The old era, the past, was the time when such divisions counted. Now, for the Christian, they no longer matter. Christ provides a new identity transcending such past and partial identities. Here too a parallel exists between the two images of new life. The end product of the melting pot was not really a true blend of all the raw ingredients but a much more definite, restricted human being. The American who rose from the melting pot was imagined as an honorary white Anglo-Saxon Protestant male; he was the true norm for the process of melting. And whatever oneness in Christ meant to Paul and his converts, it did not apparently mean an equal blending of Jew-Gentile, male-female, slave-free. These similarities between Christian and North American images of new life make the question of differences of depth and intention all the more crucial.

In order to sense these differences in more detail, let me turn to one of the most successful and contemporary expressions of the horizontal model. Indigenous to America, it depends for its plausibility on pervasive, long-lasting assumptions most of us share and replicates the myth of the fresh start in glorious form. Gail Sheehy's *Passages* uses basically the same framework for envisioning human existence that John Bunyan used, albeit with vastly different emphases and contents.

Passages: Predictable Crises of Adult Life is meant to be a book on "midlife crises," on adult development through various marked-off stages. Like *Pilgrim's Progress* it does not deal with childhood, although for a different reason. Bunyan's Baptist leanings predisposed him to restrict the Christian journey to an adults-only framework, while Sheehy assumes that adequate psychologies of childhood's predictable crises already exist. Like Bunyan's classic, *Passages* contains paradigmatic scenes where spouse and family are left behind. Unlike Bunyan, Sheehy concludes with the closure of "midlife"—in the fifties[2]—so the final passage into death is missing from her work.

The major difference between the two, however, is that whereas Bunyan is most concerned with point B, the goal, Sheehy is fascinated by the markers along the way, the points of passage or transition from one stage of development to the next. Her protagonists make their ways through age-graded transitions. They learn to build in their twenties, then leave behind what they had built during their late thirties and forties. For example, her typical adult protagonist leaves home, to head off to college or a first job or (in the case of women) an early marriage. But "leaving home" means more than geographical removal; it involves self-definition apart from one's natural milieu. An identity is created during this decade and further solidified until one's mid-thirties. Much of this identity is tied to work and career for men, family and child-raising for women. Then comes "midlife" and a shift toward new potentials. This is the time when career changes are made, when divorce and remarriage is common. A newscaster, for example, who built one life for himself, found at forty:

The whole structure crumbled. He unloaded a misunderstood wife and took on an understanding analyst. He is now living with a successful career woman his own age who makes him proud but doesn't crowd him.[3]

These departures and new beginnings are, from Sheehy's perspective, normal to adulthood in a world where change is the only constant.

It is possible to avoid these transitions, to become stuck with choices and patterns of life chosen earlier—if one lacks the courage to move on. The newscaster's wife fell into this trap. Still devoured by anger at her ex-husband, she failed to learn from her new situation. "What is the point," Sheehy wonders, "in wasting more years listlessly tossing bombs in a war that is over? Why can't she just get on with her own expansion?"[4] If Bunyan's hero was a pilgrim, intent on reaching a sacred goal, Sheehy's are travelers, trying to get the most out of each stopping place, expecting to see the territory and not stay there too long. Some of them, I fear, may be tourists—hopping from place to place, shopping and sightseeing, and confusing this with having "experienced" a great deal.

Sheehy's protagonists, like all heroes in horizontal maps, are footloose in the world. Their goal is to make the passages by confronting successfully the inner crises that biological chronology and social roles impose on them. To reach the age of forty means nothing, but to achieve with integrity the rearrangement of one's life called for by mid-life crisis is indeed an accomplishment. But the chief means of doing so is to shed previous commitments, to live out periodically in one's inner and social existence the myth of the fresh start. As Sheehy herself states, using the image of travel:

> You can't take everything with you when you leave on the midlife journey. You are moving away. Away from institutional claims and other people's agenda. . . . If I could give everyone a gift for the send-off on this journey, it would be a tent. A tent for tentativeness. A gift of portable roots.[5]

Portable roots? Is not this a contradiction in terms? No, Sheehy is saying, there are many point A's. Each stage is a beginning point, and the past becomes the enemy of the present unless one is ready to move on, to repudiate one's past for the sake of the future. Careers and marriages are begun and then dropped, as remnants of a stifling, oppressive past. New starts are not merely possible, they are mandatory. It is as if the Celestial Cities of one's youth and young adulthood become, inevitably, Cities of Destruction by mid-life. Hence Sheehy tends to minimize the amount of real suffering and grief this shedding of one's past may bring—to others as well as to oneself.

Sheehy shares with Bunyan that overall flatness that characterizes the horizontal map. Passages can be mapped in linear progression. Death lies dimly at the end of the line, cutting short one's progress in a quantifiable way. At age forty, her protagonists begin to fear death because "there isn't that much time left." The farther one moves along the line, the nearer it gets. Yet once the necessary changes are made and mid-life crises negotiated, death itself recedes as a preoccupation and Sheehy never addresses it directly.[6] Certainly Sheehy is far flatter than Bunyan, for there is no Celestial City or any other trans-earthly reality to anticipate on one's life journey. There is nothing to see through a telescope with shaky hand and dim eye. And in spite of the breezy, zippy tone used throughout, the very absence of old age and death from the book makes the journey's end in some way more subtly threatening, or at the very least restricts the traveler and reader's gaze to the markers along the way. Hence, in the landscape of *Passages* one's ultimate responsibility is to oneself: simply to get the most out of each stage and then move on.

Can we really believe that this *Passages* model of human life-mapping is anything like what baptism—as the death of the old self and the start of new life for the Christian—involves? Is to be "born again" a Christian label for this shedding of one's past, its death and burial? Is "conversion" a passage in Sheehy's sense? Sheehy's people come close to being past-less, capable of movement unencumbered by their own prior lives and commitments. Shall I interpret baptismal imagery as a symbolic promise that this mode of existence is possible and desirable? Is the "new creation" a person who can travel footloose from one place to another, considering all earlier life a succession of point A's, to be left behind? Even if this process is nowhere near so easy as Sheehy and other popular authors who use this model make it sound, is it genuinely possible at all?

I know those who would insist that it is, who see this as the fulfillment of the promise implicit in the baptismal imagery of death-resurrection and new birth. For example, the following story was used in support of just this view of newness: A thief went to prison, "met the Lord" in a conversion experience, and was then able to pass a lie detector test regarding his previous crimes. He was a "new creation," simply not the same individual who had committed the original crimes. The factual accuracy of this narrative is not at issue; its use as a model is what makes it relevant here. The man became a truly past-less person, his prior identity obliterated once and for all. No longer a thief, he began afresh, entirely freed from the past. It may be worth remarking that I did not hear this story first-hand, from the man himself, but from another person intent on using his story as a model for how God makes possible the destruction of the past.[7]

Given the vitality of the myth of the fresh start in the American context, given the plausibility of a life map such as Sheehy provides for contemporary Americans, and given the power of the New Testament imagery, it is hardly surprising that many "born-again" Christians chose to advocate this model as an ideal. To be born again in today's context means to take examples like the thief's as the paradigm for how God acts in persons' lives. Abrupt discontinuity, sudden transformation, and the dramatic defeat of vicious personal habits (such as drug use) are the hallmarks of divine intervention within this framework. Opponents of born-again Christianity have sometimes isolated this ideal and found it deplorable and dangerous. They assume that sudden transformation is per se a suspicious phenomenon and account for it as a product of brainwashing or "snapping"—alleged neurological overload.[8] Whatever limits I may see in the model of change endorsed by the myth of the fresh start, I do not mean to support any such counter-explanation. Various psychologies of conversion experience exist which do not find the phenomenon of sudden change the result of a conspiracy (as the brainwashing metaphor implies). Nevertheless, for the born-again of today, no psychological explanation could possibly replace or explain away the sense of miraculous liberation from the past expressed in the first verse of the song:

> Amazing grace! How sweet the sound
> That saved a wretch like me!
> I once was lost, but now am found,
> Was blind, but now I see.

While born-again Christians embrace the myth of the fresh start, so do some supposedly secular psychotherapies. The Human Potential Movement—the popular expression of humanistic psychology—also opted for a model emphasizing "change," "growth," and the moral necessity to liberate the self from its past. We may say that the born-again movement and its secular (or at any rate non-Christian) counterpart both employ the same model of life map. Although experienced by advocates of each as rival movements, both seem from this perspective to share many presuppositions about the possibility of change and the hope for the past's obliteration.

However, the extremity of the New Testament's imagery helps emphasize the difficulty of change. Whereas a work such as *Passages* typically makes transition a matter of changing clothes or, at most, of occasionally abandoning luggage, an image such as "new birth" really cuts through the expectation that change will be painless or easy. Rather, it *ought* to cut through such expectations. Birth is total; a completely new being appears in the world. This can't happen casually. Nor can it happen without displacing the old being who once occupied the same physical skin of the spiritual neonate.

Perhaps in a cultural climate where models of horizontal transition such as Sheehy's flourish, the fact that every new Christian birth is also a death and burial with Christ gets overlooked. We are trained to want newness without the pain of the loss of what is old, change without mourning for the past, a fresh start unencumbered by nostalgia. Hence, the revitalization of the biblical imagery of birth far exceeds the attention given today to Pauline death language.

At this point, a puzzled reader may protest. "You have made the myth of the fresh start sound like a 'myth' in the most derogatory sense, a myth as Bultmann might use that term. You have turned the hope for new life into a superficial, unreal, and naive illusion. This is simply unfair! Where would we—the human race —be without the hope for something new and alive, without the hope that tomorrow *can* be different from today? You have condemned us all to be prisoners of the past."

In reply, I can only agree that the myth of the fresh start rests on a powerful basic truth. It is not stupid, not a fictitious belief only the gullable or the foolish could hold. For it is a myth in the most profound and exalted sense, a hope that human beings cannot live without. Paul saw existence pre-Christ as ruled by "principalities and powers," the "rulers of this age" from whom Christ delivers those who have faith in him. In our era, these rulers may perhaps be construed as those forces of genetics, environment, and familial life which can and have been exalted into absolute powers. Against a view of individual existence as virtually determined by such forces, the myth of the fresh start has been, for all its limits, a vital counter-myth. Even among the most sophisticated intellectual exponents of biological and cultural determinism, the hope for an entirely fresh start retains its power—wistfully, irrationally, but deeply rooted nevertheless. And so it should: for the vision of human existence in which no newness is possible, no break with the past ever achieved, is indeed a vision of Hell, a realm of hope abandoned just as surely as the realm Dante depicted. From this vision, we may pray, "Good Lord, deliver us."

Yet the horizontal map, hopeful and persuasive as it may be, also cheats us in its very promise. To obliterate the past is neater and cleaner than to redeem it, for redemption seems to require a process more complex and painful than the shedding and repeated departures of horizontal models. To redeem was, in ancient Israel, a process of buying back and restoration, not abandonment. Its translation into Christian imagery should include these dimensions of meaning, lost in the exuberant celebration of newness that the myth of the fresh start epitomizes.

For, as if to illustrate the limits of the myth of the fresh start, there exists in contemporary life a counter-myth known to all of us: that of the amnesia victim, the truly past-less person. He or she haunts twentieth-century popular culture, a figure to be pitied, not envied. Authentic clinical cases of total amnesia are extremely rare, but the plethora of amnesia plots in literature and the arts shows the symbolic significance of this medical condition. Given the opportunity for a fresh start like no one else's, a passage to a brand-new existence, what do the amnesiac heroes and heroines of film and fiction do? They spend their entire time and energy ceaselessly searching for their past, their name, their family. Unanimously, such protagonists feel themselves cursed and incomplete as past-less persons. The same culture that upholds the myth of the fresh start, that makes it so inviting to read the newness imagery of Christian baptism as a promise of perpetual fresh beginnings, also recoils from the ultimate product of this myth. An amnesiac is a victim, not a new creation.

If this somber counter-image helps us discern the limits to the myth of the fresh start, and to the horizontal life map that accompanies this myth, we are ready to explore the two alternative models. In these we can discover how baptismal imagery finds its significance as beginning place.

6
Vertical Life Maps
and the Places of Baptism

The vertical style of life map is in many ways the most foreign to contemporary persons. Not just Dante's vision of the cosmos but almost any hierarchical order is strange to most of us. The vertical model seems, like the three-storied universe out of which it came, to be an anachronism in a day of space travel. It seems to negate just those features of the human condition that twentieth-century worldviews have so painfully stressed: the primacy of history, of existence over essence, and of change.

Nevertheless, almost surely in reaction against those worldviews, some thinkers today have turned back to vertical models for purposes other than those imagined by a Bultmann: not as cosmologies, but as inner maps, guides to the life of the soul or spirit. Within psychology, this is how the territory charted by some ancient vertical maps is being rediscovered and reexplored. Even the hierarchical structure of these maps—although not necessarily its application as a moral rating scale—is being given positive attention. Behind this renewed interest in vertical life maps lies the insight that, for some kinds of human experience, the imagery of levels works more successfully, seems more appropriate, than the horizontal imagery of stages or passages. A brief look at some current versions of these maps is warranted, before considering ways to integrate baptismal imagery into a vertical model.

Ironically, what Dante held whole has become radically split apart by the psychologists' use of vertical maps. For Dante, the Inferno and Paradise were all within one universe, comprehended in its totality by the gaze of God. In contrast, today's heirs of this model either choose to elaborate a multilevel interior Paradise or focus instead on an Underworld, an inner realm of death and darkness. When freed from the traditional tie with cosmology, these two realms can both stand as separate, and either one can offer an alternative to the imperialistic claims of earth's surface. Unfortunately, by choosing one and only one to elaborate, advocates on either side tend to ignore or reduce the realities native to the other.

The higher realm, that which Dante labeled Paradise, is the focus of interest for a movement calling itself Transpersonal Psychology. Psychologists working within this framework make the claim that the spiritual systems of the past, and particularly of the classical Hindu, Buddhist, and other mystical traditions, are in fact "psychologies," descriptions of levels of consciousness all but unknown in the West.[1] This provocative assumption allows Transpersonalists to take texts that describe many levels of meditative states as serious empirical descriptions of real, if highly unusual, mental experiences. The cosmological framework for some mystical ladders becomes accidental. The basic concern of the mystic or meditator is to chart an inner vertical journey from lower to higher levels of consciousness, a journey as orderly as Dante's trek through the medieval cosmos and as psychologically objective to those who make it.

A clear, if popularized, example of this is Daniel Goleman's *The Varieties of Meditative Experience.* The title is misleading; unlike William James, whose classic *The Varieties of Religious Experience* is evoked here, Goleman is not a pluralist. There is, he believes, one universal territory, one universal ladder of states of awareness. Various meditative systems describe and map these states in more or less detail and with more or less objectivity. Goleman uses the Theravada Buddhist text *Visuddhimagga* as a guide[2] and moves from it to other systems. The hierarchy of the Buddhist system is apparent. There are no less than eight levels of special states. Such a framework makes it relatively easy for Goleman to find comparisons between Visuddhimagga level 5 and another system's level 3. In making comparisons, Goleman must read between the lines of various descriptions of esoteric states, to conclude that basically similar experiences are being described, although the technical terminology varies from system to system. As with Dante, the higher the level, the greater its value; the levels are not (as a true Jamesian pluralist might dare to suggest) two *varieties* of experience, different but of equal worth.

Goleman, like most advocates of Transpersonal Psychology, is actually more interested in the techniques for reaching higher levels than in what one might call the "ontology" of those states of consciousness. "How to get there" is more relevant than "What is the ultimate philosophical shape of the universe as given through such experiences?" Techniques of meditation can be practiced and perfected; in fact, Transpersonalists directly teach such techniques. In this sense, the moral dimension of the hierarchy is retained. To raise one's level of consciousness is not a neutral activity, a matter of taste for a few contemplative souls and incidentally interesting for psychological study. It is a morally valued goal. "Up" carries all the prescriptive meaning it did for Dante, even more than the direction of "forward" carries for users of horizontal maps. Transpersonal Psychology such as Goleman's limits itself to higher levels and advocates a model of transcendence that is purely positive. There are, in its view, heavens—or at least the states of consciousness once turned into visions of heavens—but no hells. Some Transpersonal Psychologists are willing to consider that in the higher states one might encounter nonhuman spiritual beings, but these are almost always seen as helpful. A traditional system might easily label them "angels," but the Transpersonalist is not interested in debating their exact status or nature. Sin, damnation, torment, and death simply play no role in most of the maps of Transpersonal Psychology, although these themes may well have played a role in the experience of the original map makers, Eastern as well as Western. Overall, Transpersonal Psychology is optimistic and, in the light of William James's categories, has been called a "once-born" utilization of material probably developed by "twice-born" persons.[3]

In very radical contrast, some of the work of Jungian James Hillman provides the opposite: a vertical map without an upward direction at all. Hillman's most extravagant picture of this inner landscape is found in *The Dream and the Underworld,* a work that might well be read as a protest not only against Sheehy's horizontal vision but also against the optimism of Transpersonal Psychology. For Hillman, what Freud and Jung really discovered was "the Underworld," the realm of Hades, of darkness, sleep, death.[4] Hillman not only rejects models of inner life based around ego but also those based upon a vision of spirit and height, such as that of the Transpersonalists. "Soul" seeks depth, not height; darkness and dream, not light. Our culture is aimed at peaks, conquests, and highs; therefore it is under the dominion of the "heroic ego" and headed for self-destruction. In contrast, the realm of soul, the Underworld, is the truly radical alternative.

The Underworld as Hillman depicts it is not Hell, not a place of punishment. It is the Greek realm of Hades, the home of shades and a necessary descent from earth's surface into interiority and imagery. Everything must die out of life—earth's surface—and into soul, the realm of psychic experience with which authentic psychology and inner mapping is concerned. Therefore:

> Every resurrection fantasy of theology may be a defense against death, every rebirth fantasy in psychology may be a defense against depth, and every dream interpretation that translates images into daily life and its concerns a defense against soul.[5]

For the goal of descent to the Underworld is descent, "the radical dominion of death"[6]—not as in literal biological death but in death as a perspective intrinsic to soul. Hillman's unusual use of the vertical map therefore rejects most images of cure, growth, and progress in favor of a model of soul-making based on depth. The link between depth and evil intrinsic to most vertical maps is severed here. Unlike Dante, the Hillmanian traveler to the Underworld descends not to behold and repudiate but to abide.

These two psychological attempts to revive vertical maps are both extremely provocative critiques of normal American consciousness and the ordinary life maps it upholds. Both, for all their differences, use vertical imagery to help me see my ordinary experience anew, from a fresh vantage point. They wish to deliver me from bondage to earth's surface and ordinary, limited consciousness. Both rescue me from the flatness and banality of a horizontal map such as Sheehy's. The vertical model reintroduces the transcendence, the alternative perspective, which this flatness excludes.

Both these vertical maps transform the issue of past and present of the horizontal model into another dimension. Instead of old and new, we are offered the dualism of time-bound and eternal, of experience conditioned by history and change, and experience outside these conditions. Just as Dante's dead inhabit eternity and exist beyond the boundaries of history, so those who travel to higher levels or to Hillman's Underworld participate in a timeless mode of being, where duration has no meaning.

Read this way, the language of the three-storied cosmos, despised by Bultmann, takes on a function and a dignity that can help me speak of the role for life-mapping of similar language within Christian baptismal imagery. Thanks to the psychological theories, I can appreciate the "place" language of the New Testament as valid. Baptism as my death and resurrection with Christ brings me to the realms and places it brought him. The places of baptism—cross, tomb, the heavenly realm—can become places for me in a vertical life map. I too can move out of time and into eternity, down from earth's surface but then raised above it. From the place of burial and from the perspective of my new life "hid with Christ in God" above the earth, I am able to re-vision my earth's surface life, allow it to take on altered meaning. This experiencing of altered meaning replaces the simplistic model of the fresh start, the obliteration of the past, that was all the horizontal map could offer.

The places of Christian baptism are not—I should stress for clarity—precisely identical with Dante's Hell or with his medieval Paradise. Nor, even more obviously, are they identical with Hillman's Underworld or the higher realms of the Transpersonal Psychologists. But they are, or can become, real places, marked upon my life map, if I am willing to employ vertical categories. Moreover, today's psychological verticalists can aid me in charting these places by making clearer certain issues that are ordinarily left obscure.

One of these is the death I die in baptism. Paul's language of crucifixion and burial is so powerful, so absolute, so adamantly opposed to a hope for gradual, minimal, step-by-step transition that it seemed a perfect grounding for the myth of the fresh start. But the exact language of Romans and Colossians leaves ambiguous just "what" dies in baptism. Is it the old self? This is the meaning I have preferred.[7] But Paul actually speaks of the "sinful body" which is destroyed in baptism (Rom. 6:6), and to substitute "self" for "body" may be to overspiritualize all the death language. The death I die in baptism implicitly includes a physical association, not just an existential negation of the past. This physical connotation is made explicit by the words of the dying East African woman who said, "I go now to him whom I saw in baptism." Baptismal death is not merely symbolic if by that I mean totally apart from my embodiment. It contains within it an anticipation of my physical death.

But the physicality of death still does not account for the expanded role of death in the vertical life map. Baptismal death exists at the beginning place of my Christian life, but it also abides continuously as a possibility within that life. For in this model death is not that event which will mark the chronological end of my life, nor is it solely the end of the old which makes an absolutely fresh start possible. It abides as a dimension beneath and above all ordinary existence, an ongoing outlook beyond life. With Christ, I too have touched "the lower parts of the earth" (Eph. 4:9), where captive spirits of the dead awaited his coming. His work there was not to obliterate the realm of death and darkness but to redeem, "that he might fill all things" (Eph. 4:10). This realm of death lies just beyond the edges of earth's surface, the place of ego and ordinary consciousness.

The crucifixion and burial of the sinful self convey the sense that there exists or has existed something which is at core unredeemable, something which *must* die before redemption is possible. "Flesh and blood cannot inherit the kingdom of God," Paul wrote (1 Cor. 15:50), and whatever he meant by these words, they imply that the process of redemption requires a death. There is not enough room for God to work when an uncrucified sinful self remains alive. Whether or not we require fuller and more detailed images of unredeemable humanity, such as Dante uses, I do not know. Such images as the frozen lake at the bottom of Hell may provide a vivid picture of that which has cast itself forever beyond the scope of redemption. But perhaps truer to the intention and imagery of the New Testament is another picture: of the inhabitants of the realm of the dead, prisoners in a spiritual Auschwitz, awaiting release from their captivity. In baptism, I die with Christ—and recognize that I have been among their number.

These images, evoked by the Pauline language of baptism,

sound very foreign in a contemporary American context. That is partly because I am simply unused to the landscape a vertical map makes possible. But even more, it is because my grasp of baptism's significance has been restricted by two factors. The first is the Christian-initiation view summarized in chapter 2, which limits the context of reflection upon the rite's meaning. The second is the pervasive optimism of the myth of the fresh start. To read baptismal imagery without the latter myth requires a map other than the horizontal, however strange it may seem.

As for the heavenly realm, the realm "above, where Christ is," what can be said of this? How can this function for me as another perspective made available through baptism? Because all the biblical language is so reticent on this score, it behooves me to be extremely cautious. Even the author of Colossians, who points to the heavenly realm to redirect the Christians' attention away from "the things below," insists that the life we live within that realm is "hidden" until the day of Christ's appearing. "When Christ who is our life appears, then you also will appear with him in glory" (Col. 3:4). I would suggest, then, that to introduce this realm into one's vertical map does not automatically produce a beatific vision for all within this life. Nor need Christians be as confident as Transpersonal Psychologists that the upper realms are mappable.

Nevertheless, some access to the perspective of the self "hid with Christ" in the heavenly realm is possible. In spite of many efforts to keep mysticism out of Protestantism and out of Protestant interpretations of the Bible, the mystical ascended self is legitimately biblical, part of the vertical landscape of baptism. Moreover, in spite of all efforts to restrict Christian experience in the now to that of crucifixion with Christ and to remove all glorification language to the eschatological future, the places of baptism must include this heavenly locale if one is to be true to Pauline imagery. I feel bound to assert this, in spite of the claims of some of the most profound twentieth-century religious thought. For the latter, the asceticism of the cross must include a renunciation of all images of victory, glory, and heavenly consummation.[8] What baptism does not promise is an immediate transition to a perpetual pain-free vantage point "from above."

My aim here is to allow some room for what must be left undescribed and unexplained. The reticence of Paul about his own heavenly experiences could serve as a model, a balance between the eagerness of the Transpersonalists to provide maps and the objections of those who feel that all attempts to mention this realm, let alone map it, constitute a betrayal of the cross. To complicate this dilemma, the myth of the fresh start tends to reduce all transcendent possibilities to horizontal new beginnings along the pathways of the earth's surface. In reaction against this, movements such as Transpersonal Psychology may advocate a streamlined transcendence, a set of techniques for reaching higher levels quickly and without the pain of any prior death. Also in reaction against this, theologians may wish to dwell upon crucifixion and divine suffering, as an implicit "no" to the cheery message of *Passages* and of much popular Christianity.

A Christian heavenly perspective would be held by a self hidden with Christ. This self is not an ego writ large. But also, it is not the kind of soul Hillman advocated in *The Dream and the Underworld*—a psyche so given over to its own death and depth that it finds its goal in its own imagery, its own soul-making, rather than in Christ. Even more clearly, the self hidden with Christ cannot be the self of the horizontal model, busily traversing from point A to point B. That self has not truly died; it has merely moved on, hoping to obliterate its past in the process. As for the models of the self utilized by Transpersonal Psychology, these contain within them all the unresolved ambiguities of meshing predominantly Eastern patterns of thought and practice with a strictly Western notion of an autonomous individual oriented toward technique. In short, Transpersonal Psychology has yet to resolve the very issue, even within its own literature, with which I struggle now.

A vertical map divides time from eternity. The hidden, heavenly self lies outside time, existing beyond the edge of earth's surface and ordinary consciousness, to which it has died. But this timelessness, the vertical map's complete denial of history, has its limits. To comprehend baptism as an eschatological act, or to hope for the revealing of the hidden self, is to demand a future —and this is more than a vertical model of a life map can provide. The vertical model may be necessary in order to re-vision the realities restricted by the horizontal model, but it is not well equipped to map temporality, existence connected with past and future. The places of baptism may become more real, but the temporal structure of its imagery is obscured.

The reader may feel by this time that I have dawdled long enough with models of life maps that no one can possibly or should accept at face value. The horizontal map, based on the myth of the fresh start, simply does not meet the test of reality. Just as the American melting pot was a myth, in the sense of a false belief, and never an empirically accurate picture of immigrant life, so too the horizontal map—and the hope for complete newness—is an utterly unreal expectation. No matter how loudly some persons claim to be born again, they do not literally lose their pasts; their personalities, their social circumstances, and all the limitations of the old selves persist. To expect an obliteration of these is absurd, however vivid the imagery of new birth might be. Although persons change, "change" itself has meaning only over against what stays the same, and meaningful change simply does not work in the way the horizontal model implies.

As for the vertical model, it is just too mythic, in the more exalted, archaic sense of "myth." It seems too dependent on a sacred cosmos from the past. It requires reliance on the language of myth and seems untranslatable into more prosaic, more directly experiential terms. Transpersonal Psychologists and thinkers such as Hillman may like this feature of the model, and insist that myth is the proper mode of discourse for a truly psychic psychology, but most persons today fail to share this preference. We want a map that connects to earth's surface, to the language of ordinary life, rather than one that never departs from the esoteric higher and lower realms. The horizontal map, in the hands of either Bunyan or Sheehy, at least seems aimed at organizing the common and recognizable experiences of ambition, despair, regret, courageous determination. The vertical map seems to deal primarily with experiences intentionally reserved for an elite, or at any rate so extraordinary that they can only be charted through the very special language of myth. For this reason, I turn now to the third and most promising model of life map.

7
The Spiral Life Map

The third style of life map, which I have labeled spiral, is more complex than either of the previous ones—so much so that it requires two separate chapters to unfold fully. Here I will present some psychological theories that give the model's outline. The issues of faith and conversion do make their appearance, principally because a current theorist, James Fowler, has linked them to a partially spiral life-map model. Nevertheless, the full discussion of baptismal imagery's integration into a completely spiral model will be reserved for chapter 8. Without the psychologies of memory, of psychoanalytic theory, and of faith development, my application of baptismal death and resurrection with Christ to a third pattern of life map would not make sense.

As already mentioned, the spiral model has close connections to the literary genre of autobiography. Although not all autobiographies use this model, those labeled "autobiography duplex" by James Olney surely do. By contrast, the autobiographer "simplex" tells a tale of travel from point A to point B, a tale with a solid and given protagonist, a tale fully dependent on the horizontal life map. The autobiographer duplex is "self-conscious," and "understands . . . the sources and terms of autobiography," and knows that the work of retelling is in fact the work of creating, a work of bringing a self into being.[1] Thus the circle, as Olney believes, is the proper figure for imaginatively portraying this kind of autobiography. For the autobiographer simplex, the story can end with a point B many years earlier than the date of the writing, and the intervening years are simply dead, for the self is formed and its adventures ended. The autobiographer duplex, however, has no dead years, for the self is a-forming throughout life, and this process comes into fruition as the autobiographical work itself becomes its climax.[2]

But even the most complex autobiographies eventually conclude. In the realm of literature, the story eventually ends. The circle closes. Olney is fascinated by the revisions of earlier editions, which some autobiographers feel compelled to make, and finds the purest examples of autobiography duplex to be either those that have been repeatedly revised (Montaigne) or those written at the brink of death and published posthumously (Jung). Either case negates the possibility of dead years when the self, formed once and for all, merely continued as before.

But in most instances, there is life after autobiography. And even if no major changes of view occur, something happens to the human being whose story had already formed a circle, a patterned whole. Thus C. S. Lewis did not undergo any further conversion after he published *The Pilgrim's Regress,* but his life did not stop at this point. Instead of heading directly through the dismal swamp toward the river of death (as his protagonist did), he worked and taught and even wrote a more conventional autobiography. Then, to his own and his friends' great surprise, he actually made a major change during the last years of his life by marrying after nearly sixty years of bachelorhood. Interestingly, his wife's death three years after their marriage produced another autobiographical work, *A Grief Observed.* This, far more than *Regress,* succeeds as autobiography duplex, as he reviews his relationship with his dead wife and sees himself and his relationship to God in fresh terms. Writing *A Grief Observed* prepared Lewis for his own death.

This shift from literature to life is, then, an important qualification of our model. Literature may yield circles; lived experience is more likely to provide spirals—a series of loops backward, thrusts forward. Although at any one point the individual may "autobiographize" a patterned whole, farther along that whole is vulnerable to reworking. What held whole at one point may no longer fit. But the solution, according to this model, is not to obliterate it or leave it behind. Instead, the entire mass of experience, past and present, is re-created to form a fresh pattern. New themes, new motifs dominate. What was only recently perceived as a great moment in one's life cycle now becomes trivial or incidental or even a memory of shame. And what before had remained latent, unthematized, and of no import whatever now is viewed as a subtle but utterly critical point of transition. To use Lewis once again as an example, in *The Pilgrim's Regress* women appear as temptresses or as allegorical asexual figures (Reason, Contemplation). The hero's identity is defined without relation to any feminine figure. Yet in *A Grief Observed,* the widowed narrator recognizes that he was always a male being, always not-female, and one gift of marriage was to open him to a deeper knowledge of what being male means.[3]

The Process of Remembering

In order for this re-visioning of significant events and experiences to be possible, memory—the process of remembering— must itself work differently from what we assume. According to a popular analogy, to remember is to leaf back through the pages of an interior photograph album, to find stored therein a collection of images which, like snapshots, record exactly and unselectively scenes from the past. This, as we shall see, is an extremely misleading view of remembering as a psychological process. It is also a naive concept of photography as well. Not even photography provides us with a replica of raw reality, unprocessed. It is, even in the hands of amateurs, an artistic and personal vision of that reality, with other ingredients of the total landscape carefully selected out. I pose Uncle Ed and Aunt May in front of their trailer. I shift the camera so as to include the flower bed but not the trash cans nearby. Or I patiently wait until the baby stops crying and smiles in order to take her picture. Because we most often assume that photography is a glimpse of raw and unprocessed reality, objective in contrast to "art," the analogy of memory to photograph misleads right from the start.

What goes on when I remember? F. C. Bartlett, in his classic work *Remembering: A Study in Experimental and Social Psychology,* discovered that to remember means to schematize, to transform material seen or heard into material patterned and categorized. To reproduce from memory is, in many cases, to display the schematized product with the confidence that one has perfectly duplicated the raw material to be remembered. Bartlett showed how this process worked by asking his British research subjects to reproduce from memory several folk tales from American Indian and African cultures, stories that could not be grasped as coherent narratives without some knowledge of relevant cultural beliefs (such as ideas about ghosts and illness). Minus this knowledge, the subjects handled the task by schematizing, by taking the confusing and (to them) confused narrative and working it into a plot that did, more or less, conform to their own culture's assumptions—or at least failed to violate them as the original tales had done.[4] This was not a deliberate, self-conscious process. Bartlett's subjects, by and large, remained confident that they had accurately reproduced the original story "from memory."

This process of schematization continued as Bartlett asked for a series of reproductions. Subject B, working from Subject A's reproduction, produced a tale even less at variance with European logic and belief. The same process occurred even more dramatically when the task was to reproduce from memory confused and incoherent drawings. A "weird" birdlike drawing (based on an Egyptian hieroglyph) disintegrated into a small blob as it was serially reproduced by six subjects, then became schematized as the back view of a cat. Because the cat—two dark circles, ears, and a tail—represented a prefabricated design, an already conventional schema, it could be easily reproduced by the next eight subjects; the cat stayed constant.[5] Bartlett's studies destroy the common concept of memory as literal replication, as effortless or strained retrieval of little bits and pieces of raw reality. The mind, in remembering, does not reach back to the past as an unthematized "given" but searches through the schemas through whose aid we have retained the past at all.

Much contemporary psychology of memory involves laboratory situations, with models of remembering based on learning rather insignificant material. But studies of remembering in more natural contexts by and large reinforce Bartlett's account of things. But are *all* memories schematizations? Could some be exceptions to Bartlett's process? One interesting debate begins by reintroducing the photography analogy. Contemporary authors Roger Brown and James Kulik make the suggestion that certain memories are indeed "flashbulb memories"; they possess "a primary, 'live' quality that is almost perceptual. Indeed, it is very like a photograph that indiscriminately preserves the scene is which each of us found himself when the flashbulb was fired."[6]

The authors who coin the term "flashbulb memory" allow that

such memories are not altogether indiscriminate, but they still wish to use the photography analogy to suggest raw, unprocessed "life." (Note that the analogy avoids the viewpoint of the photographer, who may have carefully selected the scene which the subjects see as spontaneous and inclusive!) The example they chose were memories for "Where were you and what were you doing when the news came that President Kennedy was shot?" They believe that such memories trigger a Now Print! mechanism in the brain, enabling such "flashbulb memories" to stand beyond and outside the ordinary process of schematization and fading.[7]

Yet there is evidence that even the most vivid, trustworthy, and flashbulb-like memories can be completely inaccurate, fabrications fervently believed in by those who report them. At least one researcher found a Kennedy-assassination memory of this sort among her subjects, and Ulric Neisser, a critic of the concept of flashbulb memories, himself supplies another example.

> For many years I have remembered how I heard the news of the Japanese attack on Pearl Harbor, which occurred on the day before my thirteenth birthday. I recall sitting in the living room of our house . . . listening to a baseball game on the radio. The game was interrupted by an announcement of the attack, and I rushed upstairs to tell my mother.[8]

His conclusion: "Flashbulbs can be just as wrong as other kinds of memories; they are not produced by a spatial quasi-photographic mechanism." (For readers to whom Pearl Harbor is ancient history, even back in 1941 baseball was not played in December, nor was there a college or professional football game on that date that might possibly explain this fictitious memory.)

Neisser believes that the misnamed flashbulb memories are best explained as retrospective constructions, which "recall an occasion when two narratives that we ordinarily keep separate—the course of history and the course of our own life—were momentarily put into alignment."[9] They depend on a judgment of importance, a "metacognition" (an awareness about our awareness) that something with major consequences has occurred. But with this framework, we are back to the process of interpretation and the schematization of the past within the context of our own lived experience; this is the basic situation for all remembering.

Studies such as these, and also the experimental study of witnesses' testimony in the courtroom, stress the degree of historical and factual inaccuracy among even the most well-intentioned and honest rememberers. But, one may ask, how much of life requires objective, absolutely letter-perfect reproductive remembering? There are a few situations in which this is the ideal. A good witness describes the suspect accurately, without significant omissions or mistakes of detail. To remember "The Star-Spangled Banner," the Twenty-third Psalm, or the Gettysburg Address is to be able to reproduce the words exactly, to know them by heart.[10] But for most of life's tasks, we do not need this kind of memory; it is enough to have a paraphrase, a schematization, a memory that includes what for us are the key features of a situation. Were it otherwise, our autobiographies would be incredibly cluttered with pointless mental debris. Even the most enthusiastic advocates of the flashbulb and Now Print! concepts allow that very very few of our total memories are of this sort and thus seek to provide explanations for why a few are. We do not, in short, want or require an immense inner photograph album, filled with snapshots not only of Uncle Ed and Aunt May in front of their trailer but of all the clothes we have ever worn, the meals we have eaten, or the buses we have ridden. The weight of such banal events and experiences in our lives would be an intolerable burden. We desire instead a coherent narrative, a patterned whole, a meaningful past rather than a cluttered one.

But do we desire a past at all? The horizontal model, with its hope for fresh starts, suggests that a past is an ambivalent legacy, at best, and perhaps is something we can do without entirely. Looking back is, if not sinful, at least morbid or cowardly for a new creation. Experimental psychologists can offer no good reason why we should cultivate our memories, beyond the obvious practical ones: to learn more effectively and pass examinations. In cultures where oral tradition holds sway, a good rememberer plays a valuable role, as storyteller or tribal historian. Yet in Western culture, a superior memory can be an ambiguous gift. Studies of individuals with spectacular remembering ability, especially the example of Subject S studied by A. R. Luria in the Soviet Union, make this clear. S's entire experiencing was dominated by his inability *not* to remember. The result was so bizarre that his phenomenal memory seemed as much a medical symptom as a benefit to him.[11] But as we saw at the close of chapter 6, by raising the specter of the amnesia victim, we do indeed shrink from the truly past-less person, the individual who looks back and finds only nothingness. We may need a past recovered, a past reschematized, reprocessed—but without a past we exist hardly at all.

Sigmund Freud, Erik Erikson, and the Persistence of the Past

The psychology of remembering illustrates how the past becomes present for us through our own schematizing and interpretation. But perhaps the major source for the spiral model within psychology is Freudian theory. Freud's case histories follow the complex temporal format of detective stories discussed in chapter 4. Freud the interpreter-sleuth works backward from the clues of his patients' dreams and free associations to the complete reconstruction of a series of long-past events and experiences.

In the most extravagant example of this process, the case history of the Wolf Man, the patient (a young man in his twenties) told Freud of a dream he had on the eve of his fifth birthday, a dream of wolves so vivid that the patient as an adult could draw the dream scene of his childhood—a picture of five white wolves sitting motionless in a tree. The dreamer's retelling of the dream (after almost twenty years!), his associations with its images, and this picture are Freud's clues. He interprets these so as to reconstruct the five-year-old dreamer's psychological state, his anxieties over castration and his "passive homosexuality." But this reconstructed past in turn leads back to an earlier past, the original crime, so to speak, of which the wolf dream was a disguised memory. This earliest incident was "the primal scene," when the eighteen-month-old patient watched his parents' sexual intercourse.[12] The patient himself never claimed to remember this. Freud's efforts in the written case study are directed toward convincing his readers that only such an experience at so early an age could account for the dream at age five and the patient's later symptoms. Freud believes he has a coherent if bizarre narrative, rather than an inexplicable, mysterious set of unrelated events and experiences. And the reader finds it necessary to suspend disbelief, just as the reader of detective fiction must do while the story is still in progress.

But this entire procedure of psychoanalytic interpretation and reconstruction depends on Freud's contrast between the past as ordinarily, consciously experienced and the past as repressed yet unconsciously preserved. Freud's patients, so he said, suffered from "reminiscences." To move forward is to break apart the conscious images of the past, to return to the hidden and forgotten images of childhood, such as the wolves of the Wolf Man's dream. To behold these is to rob them of their power. The past when repressed poisons the individual's present existence; the past visited and made known, deciphered (especially from dreams), is forced to yield its hold over the present. The patient will no longer suffer from "reminiscences" and (like the Wolf Man, apparently) will be freed from incapacitating neurotic symptoms.

In the case histories and elsewhere, Freud uses the term "screen memory" to denote the past as falsely recalled, the consciously known past.[13] Like Neisser's erroneous "flashbulb" memory of baseball and Pearl Harbor, the screen memory will under ordinary conditions be believed, accepted, assumed to be the photographed objective image of an event long ago. Yet its meaning lies not in its objective inaccuracy but in its power to conceal the past-as-unconsciously-experienced within its imagery. Like the wolves of the patient's dream, such a memory image conceals fears, desires, and deep traces of a completely forgotten past. It is a message in code waiting for an interpreter to unlock its meaning.

To return to our photography analogy, it is as if the innocent snapshot of Aunt May and Uncle Ed did, seemingly inadvertently, include the garbage cans beside the trailer, and those cans provided an unsuspected clue to the significance of the entire scene. For in one of those cans a package could be seen, identical to one the police knew had contained cocaine. Were the picture by accident to fall into police hands, it would be a strategic clue —and a general search for dubious residents of the trailer park would result.[14] As this analogy implies, the meanings concealed are, within the framework of Freud's own writings, primarily negative, garbage cans and guilty secrets indeed.

This does not mean that Freud saw the unconscious as evil, its contents as morally wrong; his whole effort went toward bracketing that kind of judgment in an effort to grasp infantile mental life and its repression. But Freud never wrote of the recovery of the past as the quest for buried treasure or the discovery of hidden wisdom. Perhaps his patients saw their newly found, no-longer-repressed pasts as a source of power and secret strength. There is some indication that the Wolf Man was able to use the images from his wolf dream in this way. But Freud was not the slightest bit romantic or nostalgic about the lost loveliness of childhood. To recover the past is not to find one's way back to a secret realm of beauty and inner truth. What the Freudian past does reveal to each who finds it is the core of his or her own being in the sense of the root of personal suffering.

When we leave Freud himself and turn to neo-Freudian Erik Erikson, this picture changes. Erikson has revised Freudian theory but preserves the sense of the past's omnipresence within the present, its hidden grip on current life. Yet for Erikson the lost past of childhood can become a rediscovered bulwark of inner integrity, a place immune from later betrayals and ambivalences. Erikson suggests that one may draw from earliest experience a deep sense of trust in reality, a basic hope that serves as a foundation for all later development.[15] This is Erikson's view of what Freud called the "oral stage" of infantile life, when bodily pleasure and contact with the mother was established primarily through nursing. For Erikson, "incorporation" is a basic stance toward the world, one that teaches the baby how to receive from a trustworthy other. Mutuality between mother and infant, which begins here, fosters an abiding sense of trust that endures throughout life. This infantile trust and mutuality also provides an experiential grounding for much religious symbolism of loving intimacy. "Thy face, Lord, do I seek" (Ps. 27:8) would be one of countless expressions that depend upon such universal infantile experience, Erikson believes.

In Erikson's study *Young Man Luther,* this earliest experience of passive trust played a critical role in the analysis of Luther's religious and personal conflicts. The recovery of a trustful, receptive stance toward God became a means to break through the tortured young man's intense conflict with paternal authority (his father, but also God as wrathful judge) and his conscience as this authority's internal representative. Luther's Reformation made possible a new experience of intimacy with God and a new model of identity, based upon faith as personal trust, in which many others could share.[16] Erikson allows for the devastation which results when this basic early experience of being loved and nurtured is impaired, but he is nevertheless optimistic that even in cases where mistrust and anxiety have been prominent legacies of early childhood, some ego strength may be salvaged from the past.

Theories such as Freud's and Erikson's both assume that the past cannot be escaped, avoided, or obliterated. It persists within the structure of the present, just as the Underworld exists beneath earth's surface for Dante and James Hillman. Paul Ricoeur has called Freudian thought "an archeology of the subject," in which the past lies like the buried ruins of ancient cities under the town of the present. This image, which Freud himself used, helps convey the implicit hostility of Freudian thought to the myth of the fresh start. In the eyes of a psychoanalyst, all versions of the myth would be defensive denials of the past's power and its pain, escapes that are bound to fail. Those who preach the myth of the fresh start are more than likely to be unconsciously bound all the more strongly to endless repetition of the conflicts and miseries of early childhood.

Faith Development and the Spiral Model

James Fowler is a well-known psychologist of faith development who provides a theory that attempts to combine with the ideas of Erikson a basically horizontal model of growth focused on intellectual development. In *Stages of Faith,* Fowler depicts a process of growth from early childhood to advanced adulthood. Since Freud and Erikson also think in terms of stages, the use of this term in itself does not mean that a model is horizontal rather than spiral by our definitions. In Fowler's view, however, movement through stages can also be a journey in mental and spiritual growth: from simple to complex, conceptually diffuse to clear and distinct, literal to symbolic, culturally bounded to universalizing. This development is one-directional; in every case movement is movement forward. Fowler labels his stages numerically, with stage 1 in early childhood and stage 6 reached (if at all) in middle life. But although stage 6 is highest, Fowler definitely avoids a vertical model of life map altogether.

Fowler's definition of faith is not the least controversial aspect of his total project. For him, "faith" contains no definite or direct reference to transcendence. Instead, the term is meant to comprehend all aspects of the growth process, for faith is:

> People's evolved and evolving ways
> of experiencing self, others and world
> (as they construct them)
>
> as related to and affected by the
> ultimate conditions of existence
> (as they construct them)
>
> and of shaping their lives' purposes and meanings,
> trust and loyalties, in light of the
> character of being, value and power
> determining the ultimate conditions
> of existence (as grasped in their
> operative images—conscious and
> unconscious—of them.)[17]

We can see the parallel between this definition of faith and what we have been calling life map. Fowler's faith is the subjective, personal correlate of Geertz's definition of religion—and some problems arise, because of the breadth of this view and its incongruity with more conventional ideas of faith.

Fowler's stage theory resembles *Passages* in structure; his model requires a horizontal progression from stage 1 through the childhood and "conventional faith" stages. In conventional faith, one's own group norms operate semiconsciously as the arbiter of values. Faith is rarely articulated or conceptually precise; it is not thought out. Most individuals in traditional societies, and many persons in ours, remain quite placidly at this level (stage 3). In the United States they are generally Christians or nonaffiliated, while in Pakistan they would be Muslims, in Sri Lanka Buddhists, and so on—because this is what all their neighbors are. But some persons continue into the "individuative-reflective faith" of stage 4, where faith is part of an act of self-definition, of becoming an "I" over against the "they" of one's milieu. Existentialism as a popular creed sums up what stage 4 faith is all about: authenticity, rather than passive social conformity, is valued. The self has a unique destiny and holds beliefs that constitute an ideology, a clearly defined worldview. The specific tenets of this ideology may vary greatly, but Fowler notes the "how" of its appropriation, not the "what."

Yet stage 4 can be outgrown, and what follows is the "conjunctive" or paradoxical faith of stage 5. Stage 5 never is found in young adults, and its key feature seems to be a recognition of the limits of all symbolism to do justice to the realities symbolized. Such a view of symbolic language and imagery may be among the contents of stage 4's ideology, but only at stage 5 will it become a living, personal truth. The stage 5 person might be compared to the true autobiographer *duplex*, whose self is a holding whole, not simply a given. But this speculative comparison only brings home the fact that, as Fowler advances to the later, higher stages, his descriptions become more precarious. This is abundantly true when he comes to the "universalizing faith" of stage 6. This is the level reached by the world's great religious and moral teachers, who serve as exemplars of a universal, actualized, and self-transcending humanity. Fowler provides no interview examples of this kind of person, and it is hard to avoid the impression that stage 6 is more a spiritual ideal (albeit a very fine one!) than an empirically observed phenomenon.[18]

As with *Passages,* one may grow physically older in Fowler's life map without making the psychic transition. And there is absolutely no doubt that, within the terms of this model, stage 6 is "better" than the earlier stages. The pathetic cases of chronologically mature adults who still function at levels 2 and 3 show that Fowler's horizontal model is as morally evaluative as Dante's system. He wants everyone to get at least to stage 4, and he hopes to stage 5 (stage 6 may be too much to expect!)

But Fowler is enough of an Eriksonian, and indebted enough to the Freudian tradition, that he must acknowledge that the past does not get left behind with stage 1. Each stage is a reworking of both present and past and requires just the kind of spiral, reflective return to the images of the past that we have identified as the hallmark of the spiral model. In fact, within the context of a discussion of conversion, Fowler provides the clearest possible support for this model, in the form of a spiral-shaped diagram to illustrate "Conversion and Recapitulation of Previous Faith Stages in Healing and New Growth."[19] And when he offers a lengthy and detailed case history, "Mary's Pilgrimage," to illustrate his theory of faith development, Fowler's Eriksonian and therefore Freudian loyalty outweighs his focus on progressive horizontal stages.

In the treatment of conversion, and especially with this case history, I can see the same uneasy conflation of two independent models that we saw in C. S. Lewis's *The Pilgrim's Regress*. There is also the additional problem caused by a definition of faith that does double duty: once as a term almost synonymous to our "life map" (Fowler's own definition) and once in its more ordinary sense of explicit religious commitment.

In the case study, Mary is a convert to a Christian group that relies on the imagery of new creation. But Mary's problems do not vanish with her conversion. She creates misery for herself and others, is given guidance both good and bad, and marries a man as unstable as herself. Finally, after a divorce and several geographical moves, she settles down and appears to gain some peace and maturity. Fowler sees one source of her problems in that her form of Christianity

> interpreted her new being in Christ as arising out of the cancellation of her old being. This meant the cancellation of what I have called the "willful self"; it also meant the obliteration of her past. . . . Because of the pain and chaos in the past—particularly in the recent past—the new convert welcomes this obliteration. . . . To acknowledge that the past, in its pain and grief as well as its times of grace and gladness, still is present in the psyche and is part of the person's ways of seeing and responding to life is threatening.[20]

As an heir to Freud, Fowler cannot believe in the obliteration of the past, and his adherence to Erikson permits him to hope that "grace and gladness" can be found alongside the pain and grief of the past. He therefore continues:

> The problem of this strategy of obliterating the convert's past life is that it short-circuits the conversion process. . . . After a time of radical discontinuity with her past . . . Mary could be led . . . into a healing recapitulation of the earlier stages of her life. . . . Conversion, to be complete, involves a revisiting, a revalencing and recomposing of the stages of one's past faith in light of the new relationship to God brought about in the redirecting phases of the conversion. Ego psychologists speak of "regression in the service of ego development." I prefer the concept of recapitulation.[21]

In this quotation, we have an eloquent rejection of the myth of the fresh start and of those horizontal models of life map which encourage the hope that the past can and should be obliterated.

But there are at least two substantive problems raised by this. First, nothing in the overall theory of faith development laid out by Fowler in the main sections of *Stages of Faith* really supports the value of earlier life stages. One is expected to move through them, leave them behind. Why should the person at stage 4 attend to stage 3? What could it offer? Second is the confusion caused by Fowler's definition of faith when it is automatically applied to the start of religious faith in the more conventional (albeit restricted) meaning of the term. Only for Fowler's definition did the pre-conversion Mary have "faith," and therefore only he can speak of conversion as a "revalencing and recomposing" of "one's past faith" rather than as the *beginning* of faith. Fowler as an Eriksonian wants the past abiding within the present, and he also wants faith as a continuous human potency active even in earliest life. But like Mary and her fellow Christians, the rest of Fowler's theory supports a horizontal model of growth in which the past, if not quite obliterated, is easily left behind. In this latter model, faith defined as overt religious commitment can enter at any point along the journey, the start of one's relationship to God and not merely its redirecting or becoming conscious.

At the root of Fowler's complaint against the myth of the fresh start in a case like "Mary's Pilgrimage" is that it demands "the denial of self when there is no selfhood to deny."[22] Mary's legacy was one of pervasive mistrust, going back to earliest infancy. In a sense she had not been fully born from woman, and so her new birth as a Christian convert was, Fowler believes, flawed from the start. To die to self, one must first have "a sinful body," a self one can call one's own: this is to say, an adult identity, however imperfect.

Within the context of Fowler's stage theory, one might see this as a sign not only that the Pauline and Johannine baptismal imagery was designed for adult converts but also that it was developed by persons who had reached stage 4 faith at the very least. At this stage one can differentiate one's own map of reality sharply from that of the social, cultural, and familial milieu. In short, "death of self" and "new birth" are meant for persons who, unlike Mary, have identifiable, strong selves to lose and whose surrender of these selves to God is not based upon the pain and chaos of low ego strength. This is the implication of Fowler's position.

This solution, offered by Fowler in his Eriksonian mode, is directly endorsed by others working within the neo-Freudian perspective of religious psychology. It implies something that is obviously psychologically plausible and confirmed by many religious counselors. Only those with strong identities, positive legacies from early childhood, are capable of the kind of self-yielding that the death of the self with Christ requires. In the words of John McDargh:

> The same conditions which cause an individual to hold back from the risk of interpersonal intimacy and self-donation are at work in the fear and mistrust which resists the transforming reception of God's *agape*. . . . Our sense of ourselves as available for . . . "loving self-donation" never proceeds from a deprivation or an inner emptiness, but rather from a taste of the satisfaction in sharing. . . . Without that basic inner sustainment of which the psychoanalysts have tried to speak, the person is not wholly available for self-donation.[23]

Psychologically plausible, yes—but one spiritually dubious consequence is hidden here. According to this neo-Freudian view of faith and development, those with primarily negative pasts, those like Mary who lack a strong identity to surrender, will be, in subtle ways, unfitted for the *new* identity available in Christ. McDargh suggests this as a psychological variant of "To the one who has, more shall be given him, and to the one who has little even that little shall be taken away" (Matt. 25:29).[24] But to me this turns an admittedly hard saying of Christ into a very dubious judgment. For it implies that the Marys of the world are doubly cursed: once by a childhood that leaves them maimed and yearning for its obliteration, and then again by a spiritual system most inappropriate for persons with such impairments—a system which, when they seek to receive its benefits, will only compound their grief. If stated this starkly, the implications of the Freud-Erikson-Fowler vision of the past's power become spiritually disastrous.

Why so? First, because the message of the Christian gospel was and is intended for all, but especially for the poor, the oppressed, and all those burdened and imprisoned by sin in all its forms. It is precisely to the Marys of this world that Christ came to bring hope—not to those better-suited to salvation through fortunate early experiences, and so in no need of a physician. The theories of depth psychology, which take the power of the past most seriously, can, when used in conjunction with a Fowlerian understanding of faith, turn ego strength into a kind of prerequisite for salvation. Does availability for "loving self-donation" precede God's grace in the individual's life, or does it issue from it as a fruit? If Christian faith requires this capacity in order to work, is a second Savior needed to meet the needs of the really incapacitated? For all Christians, such an option is ruled out, as are any human prerequisites for salvation through Christ. Yet potentially—however unintended—Fowler's kind of theory produces a twentieth-century psychological version of salvation by personal aptitude, if not quite by works.

Second, to stress the power of the past is not to grant it absolute power to determine, omnipotence against which no future influences can possibly triumph. Even Freud, that strict psychological determinist, was not deterministic in this sense, or the very process of therapy itself would be undermined at the start. However pessimistic, Freud retained the hope that it was possible "to exchange hysterical misery for common unhappiness," as he wrote to a prospective patient.[25] Those who misunderstand Freudian thought about the past bolster their own "hysterical misery," clinging to it as an absolutely fated and unchangeable legacy. Those who find the past too powerful to fight have badly misused the theory. The original hope of psychoanalysis was the defeat of slavery to reminiscences, not support of their continued rule. If this can be said about Freud's ideas, then it can certainly hold in regard to the claims of neo-Freudians. And if this is true about the reduction of the past's power within the most secular psychotherapeutic context, it ought to be even more true whenever there is a Christian appropriation of such theories. For Christians, the old age and its powers cannot be ruling still. Even in the interest of a definition of faith that links adult present to early infancy, this triumph of Christ over the rulers of this age should not be forgotten.

In the next chapter, I will spell out how such spiral models as I have described here might incorporate baptism, re-visioning its role and, in turn, letting its imagery aid in the re-creation not only of the Christian's past but also of the present.

8
The Redemption of the Past

Having drawn together the psychological framework for a spiral model of a life map, let us now specify how baptismal imagery can be joined to such a pattern. The processes of construction and interpretation give access to the past through memory. All the developmental theorists insist upon the need for the backward loop in the spiral, for what Fowler called the "recapitulation" of the past. We also saw how some advocates of a spiral model applied it to individual Christian existence, to claim that the possibility of faith is rooted in the remote past of childhood. Only through a constructive recapturing of this past will the trust and "loving self-donation" of faith become actualities. Whatever the problems with this model, it cannot be said to demand the obliteration of the past, as did the horizontal life map, nor is it so distant from ordinary earth's surface experience as is the vertical map.

Can I now link to Christian baptismal imagery what both Bartlett and the depth psychologists have discerned about the nature and meaning of the past? This imagery provides access to that realm of spiritual geography which meets and changes my individual life map. Through it, I am given a fresh relationship between my past, present, and future. I will re-schematize the past, encountering it now not as I once did, when it was the present, but as it now is discerned in relation to my life in Christ today.

For the Pauline imagery of baptismal death, burial, and resurrection with Christ, the death I too die is a liberation from the sin and from the inner death I carried along within my past self. The point of burial is actually a point of release, "For he who has died is freed from sin" (Rom. 6:7). To die in this manner is to be released from the hold of the past, to undo the work of sin as it has locked me in its grip. It is a new birth and a fresh start. From this language, we saw how easy it was to hope that I can indeed obliterate the past; hence the optimism of the horizontal model. At the same time, in spite of Paul's "once and for all" language, I realistically know that as the sinful past it continues to abide within me, experientially present as that which should have died in baptism, but did not.

But recall how complex the past is for a truly spiral model! The past is *not* a private snapshot album, but a story I tell. It draws upon events but is capable of being retold, reschematized. What gets obliterated in my baptismal death with Christ is not *the* past, in its simplistic chronological totality—the entire inner photo album—but *a* past, a past based upon a particular set of schematizations. This is the past my old sinful self required, the past it constructed and maintained. But now it must die with Christ, as an intrinsic element of that self who dies with him. For if we take the evidence of Bartlett and other psychologists of remembering seriously, the past is a processed vision of myself and never merely a replication of a set of raw happenings.

The Freudian and neo-Freudian psychologies insist that there is always an unthematized, unconscious past, lurking partially disguised behind the conscious past and its screen memories. This concealed past may be by its very nature too complex and too painful to be captured adequately within any one narrative, and certainly it exceeds the past of everyday remembering. Yet it can become a source for new schematizations, new constructions—for a new, more profound and inclusive sense of my own inner and unique history.

I believe baptismal imagery makes possible this process, empowers it by offering an imagery suitable to apprehend it. The death I die with Christ is a place where the schemata of my remembering are surrendered. There in Christ's tomb they are done to death and I am released from their hold. These schematizations were the screen memories that conveyed what I believed to be my one and only past. They made up the story I told myself about who I was and what I had experienced. This story I assumed to be beyond doubt, the way things really were—that is, until I let the waters of baptism dissolve this past. The cross and tomb of Christ reveal it for a construction, crucify and bury it.

Through the death of this constructed past, the forces at work in its building are revealed to me as those which Paul called "the law of sin and death." Behind the screen memories lie far more painful rememberings from which the screen memories protected me. To die to my screen memories is to admit that the deeper past they hid must indeed have been a past of sin and death, a past whose full anguish I now confront for the first time. Nor is the sin and death in my past limited to my own attitudes and acts; I discover myself as one who collaborated with the sinful existence of others. Whether as uninnocent victim or as accomplice, I discover my solidarity in sin as a member of family and society. Precisely this agonizing confrontation is what a recapitulation of the past requires—the same recapitulation that Fowler saw as the completion of the conversion process. Such a meeting with the past of sin and death is painful enough to make the baptismal language of crucifixion and death vividly real.

To follow through the implication of this, I need to cling closely to Pauline imagery. Only what has once lived can truly die. The past I had schematized and carried within me as "my past" had lived, so to speak—therefore it can be crucified and laid in the tomb with Christ. This I may call my first past, my *known* past. It may be a past filled with vague guilts, blurred shameful memories, and unresolved tensions—but it is the past I know. In contrast, the unconscious, hidden past has never truly lived, never been permitted full access to my awareness, and never been merged into the fullness of my individual life map. It has indeed existed, in a shadow state like that of the Underworld, unable either to reach the earth's surface or truly to rest in peace. From this shadow existence I must call it forth into life, if only to free it to die in its turn.

This shadow past is a second past and is never so clear and distinct as the fully schematized first past. It is composed of that which the first past could not include or understand, of those vague or brooding but blurred elements within the first past. I should not assume that it is necessarily more evil than the first past, but it is more mysterious and more threatening. Otherwise, it would not have had to sink down below consciousness long ago. And what the first past left murky may become all too crisply outlined and illuminated in the second past. I may have, through the first past, nursed a grievance against a parent—but only at the level of the second past can I see and admit the extent to which

I was a victim of both parents, whose hurting, fragile identities I was meant to support.

Moreover, if I can now see the first past as a product of my own schematization, then so too is the second past, the past that I come to know with the defeat of the first. There is no reason for me to treat the newly exposed unconscious memories as flashbulbs, photographs of uninterpreted, raw reality—although the events I schematize may be historically accurate. Freud may have claimed to discover totally buried primal scenes of parental intercourse observed, but recall that the primal scene could never be retrieved directly from the memories of the Wolf Man.[1] In some sense, it remains a reconstruction of Freud, the detectivelike interpreter of his patient's memories. But even the patient's own postpsychoanalytic rememberings are themselves a fresh set of schematizations. This set is inclusive of the grief and anxiety of the past's events as these were once apprehended, but they are no less schematizations.

The second past differs from the first because it includes the griefs, fears, and hurts of the past's events. It is this second past that Mary, Fowler's convert subject, fled from, attempting to obliterate all past and so die to a life that had never been lived in the first place. She tries desperately to abandon an identity she never possessed, for to possess an identity within this spiral model demands a self schematized as inclusively as possible, fully allowing the negative experiences of one's earlier life. The backward loop of the spiral gives vitality to this shadow past, this second past. This in turn opens the future, a true future that is more than moving on, burdened by the invisible luggage of the un-dead past.

But must the second past die in baptism in its turn as well? Or do we through it receive our new life, the life alive to God in Christ Jesus? Is the second past in some way to be equated with this new life? Let me translate this question into more conventional psychological language and then show what is at stake in it. According to Fowler, the recapitulation of the past will in fact yield "times of grace and gladness" as well as a deeper awareness of one's own pain.[2] For in early experience lies a positive foundation for later ego strength and identity. But if Fowler's theory requires this, I may still ask, "*Do* I find 'times of grace and gladness' in the second past, as a foundation of trust which even the pain and chaos cannot shake or erode?"

Erikson, Fowler, and McDargh assume a pattern that emphasizes this discovery as the grounds for faith. The explicit faith of
a convert arises out of a very early indigenous faith, from which
my adult capacity for "loving self-donation" emerges. Fowler's
recapitulation connects early and current forms of faith in consciousness. Hence, paradoxically, the "new life in Christ" would
be my own oldest, earliest, most fundamental life—life experienced in the mutuality of infantile trust. In this sense, Fowler
and McDargh would answer the opening questions of the previous paragraph by affirming that the second past need not die. For
through it I find a core of selfhood that connects me in faith to
Christ.

But must there lie behind my first past, deep within the second
past, such a solid core of positive experience, a nucleus regaina-
ble and forever beyond betrayal by what comes later? Is the
redemption of the past to come through my finding of such an
inviolate early core, at the further point in the backward loop of
the spiral? And, even if I do discover this, shall I, like Fowler and
McDargh, see in such a legacy the original form of personal
faith?

There is evidence that at least some persons construct their life
maps this way. They retain vivid but elusive memories of some
childhood moment of grace and gladness and years later describe
"a return in the sense of a rediscovery of a truth once known and
long hidden."[3] One may find many examples of this in a fascinat-
ing collection of childhood religious experiences, Edward Robinson's *The Original Vision*. Here, adults recall such long-lost
experiences and provide support for this feature of the Fowlerian
spiral model. These experiences include the mysterious and awe-
inspiring, the beautiful and sublime—and typically it is not until
mid-life that persons learn how to return to them, to know that
in such memories they have touched something ultimately real
and beyond later betrayals and false forgettings.

If I indeed find in the past such a hidden core of unspoiled
integrity, the redemption of my entire past will depend on making this original vision the center of a fresh set of schematizations. I will tell a fresh narrative of new life which draws implic
itly upon the old, to complete the loop of the spiral and send me
forth into the future. I will have gained not happiness, necessarily, but meaning, that precious sense of life as a patterned whole
to which Olney testified. For me, then, the life lived to God in

Christ will incorporate, of necessity, such latent but valuable memories from my personal past as can provide a firm grounding for an existence held whole. Conversely, no presentation of God or Christ—however theologically correct—has a chance to gain my true assent so long as it remains disconnected from this inner core of memories.[4]

These deep memories, previously hidden resources, can now be freshly schematized, integrated, and included within an over-all identity "in Christ." To become a new creation in this process is to transmute the old, to buy it back from enslavement to a now-abandoned narrative of myself. But although the old has passed away—my first past has died with Christ—at least a part of it, the "second past," has been received into a new existence, re-created and fitting for a new and more inclusive identity.

Here I have indeed one possibility for the past's redemption. But there is a less appealing and hopeful alternative. Suppose that what I find, even after the deepest and most intense search through the past, is no untarnished, unblemished core. Instead I find the absence of such an original vision as Robinson's subjects report. I may discover that no matter how hard I search I cannot find unbetrayable trust or a time of grace and gladness rooted in my earliest existence.

Is this second alternative possible? I believe so. Against all the theories which support, however tentatively, an image of early innocence and bliss, I risk discovering only the trauma of birth from woman, sullied and filled with pain and weeping. Instead of an original home in Paradise, I find instead the exile and its effects—the traces of primordial, original sin. In short, to borrow Fowler's language but in reverse, I may find "unfaith" as my primary early reality, an inner human capacity prior to any con-scious rejection of God.

Such a bitter alternative leaves me bereft of certain key psycho-logical resources for a secure identity, for a fresh start and for faith as this might be understood within Fowler's version of the spiral model. I would discover—to use McDargh's biblical cita-tion—that I was among those who "had not," and so what little I thought I had was now taken from me; while to others more graced by early environmental factors, these needed foundations of trust and selfhood, the prerequisites of faith, would have been given. This dismal but plausible alternative, contrasting vividly to the hope implicit in the theories of Erikson and Fowler, must be seen as a real outcome for one who explores the second past. This shadow past is made accessible only upon the death of the first past, my more bearable set of screen-memory schematizations. It cannot be guaranteed in advance to contain within itself resources for hope and faith.

Now, an advocate of Fowler's view might object, "This grim alternative you just described is an entirely fictitious one. All but the most severely disturbed and profoundly impaired persons *do* recall some core of trust, goodness, and love, something to serve as the foundation for later identity and future expressions of faith." Indeed, it is probably the case that relatively few persons emerge from childhood with *none* of these experiences. Yet empirical studies such as Robinson's show that not all adults can use childhood as a foundation for trustworthy authentic selfhood.

Is this because many persons have miserably unhappy nightmarish childhoods, filled with fear and chaos and loneliness? Perhaps. Nevertheless, psychotherapists are reluctant to assert a clear one-to-one relationship between the objective evils of any individual's early life and the degree of his or her adult neurosis.[5] Perhaps the actual quality of the past is less the issue; what becomes critical is my capacity to schematize, to make my past serve as a positive foundation. However, to say of myself, "I lack the capacity to make my past a positive source for my present," is to return to the issue of my own inner capacities—or lack thereof. So let me take this pessimistic alternative view of the past as bereft of resources seriously. If I do, I will seek a model of its redemption other than Fowler's. If my hope for a previously hidden but really trustworthy foundational core of faith from my own past has been disappointed, my second past is revealed as ultimately in need of even more redemption than the first.

Here, I believe, the baptismal image of new identity in Christ, of new life which is "hidden in Christ," guides me to respond to this bleak discovery in hope. For it is no longer in myself but in Christ that I find my life. To assert that I live postbaptism in Christ means that I can receive through him from God the core of trust, integrity, and love that I have failed to discover within the depths of my own past. What, under other more favorable conditions described by Erikson and Fowler, might have been given through childhood and its early experiences schematized as memory, I now must receive later in life and more directly from God. Because the identity I have postbaptism is one I share with Christ, Christ can accomplish what my own past could not, after all, provide. The redemption of the past, its buying-back from sin and death, will occur as Christ's faith, love, and identity become the basis for new schematizations. Christ, and not childhood experience, becomes the foundation for my identity. The law of those who have little and those who have much is overcome by a God who desires to give even to those who have absolutely nothing of their own.

Curiously, when this redemptive process happens, I can accept that the pain, grief, and fear of the past—the exile instead of the Garden—is still worth my having experienced. For this version of the spiral model permits me to come into possession of the patterned whole of the circle just as surely as does Fowler's. This circle has a perfection very unlike that meant for angels, who know nothing of pain, loss, or mistrust. But it holds whole nevertheless. Such a circle depends upon the intervening and redeeming activity of Christ, its true center. It does not depend primarily upon the givens of early experience or a faith that is contingent on such experience.

But the same, I believe, can ultimately be said for the first model of the past's redemption. The capacity to reschematize, to uncover what was buried and face the past's pain, is already a capacity granted to Christians through Christ's life and activity in their own lives. To be able to find some trustworthy core within the past already presupposes that I have received both the grace and the courage to break through the false first past and search for it.

Therefore, I need not make too sharp the contrast between the neo-Freudian model, with its trust in the "good past," vs. a model of a past bereft of grace and gladness. Nor, I believe, is the choice ever one of deciding between a human vs. divine origin for the work of redemption. For both variants of the spiral model, the possibility of the spiral back to the past and the hope of the past's redemption are gifts of God. God has provided both and is free to give within the boundaries of individual capacities and beyond them.

Should these two possibilities for the spiral model of life map be seen in the light of a major religious division? Is the Erikson-Fowler alternative in some sense a Catholic pattern, in that it emphasizes the continuity between nature and grace, between human capacity for faith or "loving self-donation" and God's action through that capacity as given in infancy? On the other hand, is the alternative pattern that I have called the pessimistic alternative of the bleak and untrustworthy past a typically Protestant one? The latter focuses upon discontinuity between yearning and reality, between human incapacity and divine action, between childhood unfaith and Christ's identity as the source of all true faith. It depicts a flawed human order and a divine reversal of it. McDargh, writing on this issue, leaves room for such a contrast. Interestingly, virtually all the neo-Freudian psychological materials he employs intentionally stress continuity[6] and so, by the above criterion, would be Catholic in emphasis.[7]

I find it important to insist that both models, both possible patterns, require the activity of God and the new identity in Christ. Whatever one's position on nature and grace, the presence of God and his activity as the ultimate source for all schematizing of my past is the true prerequisite for the past's redemption. Nevertheless, the model I have labeled pessimistic simply makes this more explicit. It somehow fits the pattern of baptismal imagery more intensely.

In both these patterns, the past is redeemed, yet in both it dies. As a narrative composed of schematizations, it is always vulnerable to future deaths and in need of future redemption. The process I have described is not a once-and-for-all event but a recapitulation I can repeat as a series of loops in a spiral. Each time, the previous schematizations will be brought to the burial place, which becomes for me the place of liberation from their stranglehold. Each time, I emerge more fully alive in Christ, with a more inclusive and adequate narrative of my own past.

For this reason, baptismal death and resurrection within the spiral model of life map is never merely a point A from which I immediately move forward. Baptismal imagery provides a place that anticipates future spiraling, a place to which I can and must return. Again and again, I must be prepared to lay in Christ's tomb those schematized versions of the past that need to die with him in burial. In hope, I await God's act in raising up a self in possession of a new vision of past and identity. In this sense it is a beginning place, a place of creation and re-creation. Whether I first entered it as infant or adult, its imagery provides a model for what will take me all my life to fulfill. And each time, when I return to it, in my journey back into the loop of the past, I will see it and know it more truly than I did before.

9
Baptismal Imagery and the Future

Where does the future fit within the life-map perspectives we have explored? So far, baptismal imagery, and its meaning for individual life-mapping, seems focused upon the problematic past and its abiding reality for postbaptismal existence. With the three models, I showed the variety of ways the imagery of death and resurrection with Christ proper to baptism can be read as a pattern for each individual Christian's life map. As the models grew more complex, so the meaning of "past" grew less obvious, until the idea of a single snapshot-album *given* past was discarded. If "past" has yielded several meanings—such as the contrast between first and second pasts, the conscious past and the shadow past—perhaps the meaning of "future" is also not so obvious.

We recall that baptism as Paul and the other New Testament writers conceived it was an eschatological act, a rite pointing toward the expected future consummation of God's kingdom, marked by the return of Christ at the last day. To die Christ's death, and be raised with him, is a pattern of imagery with importance not only for the now and present life but for a *not yet*. When "resurrection now" is portrayed as the postbaptismal state of the Christian (as in Colossians and Ephesians), there is still room for this eschatological future. On the day when the hidden Christ is revealed, in that *then* I too will no longer be hidden from myself and will share in Christ's glory. This future was to be a cosmic transformation worked by God. So sure was Paul of this hope that it barely mattered whether it was fulfilled before or after his individual death.

Eschatology in this precise form is almost impossible for me to recapture or duplicate. It is quite absent from virtually all the psychological sources I have used. There is instead available to me a centuries-long focus upon individual death as the major future of interest to Christians. The Last Day that counted for Paul gave way to a concern for "the hour of our death," especially at the beginning of the age of individualism.[1] Some agree with Oscar Cullmann that this shift meant the betrayal of a Hebraic vision of collective resurrection in favor of an utterly individualistic hope drawn from Plato and not the Bible, hope for disembodied immortality.[2] Others believe these two expressions of hope are more closely intertwined, and perhaps both are legitimate alternatives.[3] But the fact is, for the majority of Christians, John Bunyan's Celestial City represents the future promised in baptism. This goal is available only after my death and is in no way guaranteed to me, even after I have crossed the river at the edge of this life and left the world of pilgrimage behind. Without this goal, the landscape of *Pilgrim's Progress* would be a meaningless series of disconnected dangers, nor would the hero have had any reason to leave his home in the City of Destruction in the first place. The Celestial City completes the traditional horizontal map, gives it its structure. However, it is just this structure which no psychological version of a horizontal life map cares to duplicate.

The traditional vertical map was well adapted to an exclusive emphasis on individual immortality. Dante's realms above and below were—are—eternal, but each individual moves decisively into one of them upon death. These realms, timeless and ever-present, lie outside the boundaries of ordinary existence for the living. Each person's choices in life will bring him or her to one of them: to writhe in despair and misery, to submit to purgation, or to rejoice in blessedness. Our fulfillment as human individuals thus lies beyond the realm of earth's surface. Death is not primarily the final stage of a journey; in death, accidentals are stripped away so that the person, perceived eternally as God perceives him or her, will come to be only what he or she most truly is. As each soul moves out of time and into eternity, it gains this new relation to its own essence. This happens after death—but in the timeless realms, "after" and "before" no longer mean what they do to the living. Recall that the dead inhabitants of all three Dantean realms mingle in a hodgepodge of historical periods and cultures. The figures of classical epics rub shoulders and share torments with the recently dead of Florence.

The contemporary psychological attempts to revive the vertical model make no attempt to reconnect it with a postdeath future existence. The Transpersonal Psychologists were interested in levels of consciousness, some of which seemed to exalt the person into a state transcending time; hence the entire question of life *after* death would become misstated and misconceived. Others, especially those who rely on explicitly Eastern models of the various levels, also adopt the framework of karma (fate) and rebirth, which traditionally accompanies the meditation systems which interest them. In Westerners' eyes, hope for reincarnation simply extends the scope of the horizontal map, as well as buttressing the myth of the fresh start in a way not permitted by Christianity.

Hillman's approach, on the other hand, did very explicitly link the Underworld with death and saw death as the "telos" or goal of every soulish image. Yet Hillman's goal is to deliteralize death, restoring death as a dimension of soul and depth instead of reducing it to a biological, clinical problem. This detemporalizes death, robs it of any intrinsic connection to the future. Moreover, Hillman writes as if it is the ego for whom the future is necessity, for whom the future is territory that must be conquered. The realm of soul, the Underworld, is basically beyond personal time entirely, yet subtly linked to the collective past. It is a realm of primordial realities, a heritage already given, far more than it is a promise of future revelation.

With the spiral map, the central image is that of a circle whose circumference surrounds a patterned and meaningful whole. This image dramatically reveals the inner structure of great autobiography. Yet when we examined psychological frameworks for the spiral model, it became apparent how concerned such models are with the problems of childhood and memory. They are marginally focused upon the future in any form. Each backward loop of the spiral is necessary for an advance, yet the goal of the spiral movements is not stressed. Or, as in Fowler's theory, a spiral model is placed in uneasy collaboration with a horizontal one. The future here, as with Sheehy, is psychological and religious maturity, not chronological aging. Perhaps the future will be a universalizing faith (stage 6), which, however, very few achieve.

But this review of how the three models deal with individual death leads me back to the shift from the Pauline "day of Christ" to the hope for personal immortality. Is individual death, *my* death, the only future relevant to baptism? Or is it at best a symbolic intimation—and at worst a self-centered substitute—for the future of the Eschaton, of God's complete consummation of the great plan of redemption? What other vision of the future dimension of baptism can be provided, which does not merely substitute my destiny for that of all creation? Which image can, one hopes, be congruent with the spiral model's complex revisioning of existence?

Before I suggest some ways to imagine such a relation, I can describe how the death I die with Christ in baptism can become a paradigm or pattern for biological death at the chronological end point of my life. The One seen in baptism will be the One seen in death. Although baptism is not full salvation, the beginning of Christian life implicitly contains its end. Because of this, even within the horizontal life map, baptism might become a model for a Christian death. I learn to die in baptism, at point A in my journey—and this knowledge is of ultimate value, not only at the start but at the very brink of the point B that marks the journey's end. Recall that although baptism went unmentioned in *Pilgrim's Progress,* the transition from this life to the next was symbolized there by submersion in water. Just as Christ was raised from the dead, and I with him once before, so at the brink of death I may anticipate the repetition of this pattern, in the same faith I held before.

Already, however, the spiral model has impinged on this formulation of hope at the point of death. The end and the beginning come together; the two immersions are really perhaps one. Instead of simply an experience at point A from which I learn what will later be of great use, I find that points A and B collapse upon each other. The One first seen in baptism can be there at the close of the journey because I will have come full circle and can see more clearly him whom I found there long ago. Baptismal death is not merely an anticipation, it includes in its imagery all my deaths, even that physical one at the chronological end of my life. And perhaps once I have arrived at this formulation, I may recognize that "my" individual physical death is no longer the ultimate point B which most horizontal maps make it out to be. Christian life could be re-visioned as a circle centered in God, with deaths—baptismal, physical—the entranceways into God. Neither death nor self are by themselves the goals, and the self who dies is both decentered and reborn as it finds itself in God.

When we have said this, are we ready to imagine each individual death as meaningful within a much larger framework of death and new life lived to God? Within such a framework, my own existence in its lived wholeness can become, like baptism, a symbolic eschatological act, whose meaning points toward the fulfillment of God's redemption. That this redemption is visible in me only very weakly and obscurely will not invalidate such a perspective on my life as a totality. The journey I take in time can become a microcosm of the immense journey of all things toward their restoration in God.

A horizontal map can attempt to express this hope through the symbolism of cosmic, universal evolution. The cosmic journey may spread out over millennia but nevertheless be a real and inevitable progress toward the divine telos. Evolution is goal-directed here, growth toward a fulfillment rather than a random series of natural experiments. This vision is mythic just as surely as the three-level universe of the vertical map is mythic; in spite of its scientific or semiscientific vocabulary, it belongs outside the realm of natural science. As mythic vision, it extends and universalizes the scope of the horizontal map. It holds out the hope of a universe in which all things find their fullness in God, and God will be at the end—in Paul's words—"everything to every one" (1 Cor. 15:28).[4]

But there are problems with this vision. A horizontal map—unlike the vertical—must take history into account as the real arena of God's redemption. When it is my individual history, I face with Bunyan's protagonists the fearful knowledge that there is a door to Hell even at the gates of the Celestial City. The same caution must apply whenever this model is extended to a more collective, universal, and ecological scope for a divinely given future. Redemption is not so inevitable, so guaranteed, as the metaphor of evolution permits one to hope. The optimistic inclusiveness with which this language of progress is often used helps us forget that, in actual biological evolution, a great many life forms perish. There are species that are evolutionary dead ends, and there is no advance guarantee that any one species will survive over very long-term periods of geologic and climatic change. Moreover, the last day of the physical universe as a whole may be marked by the triumph of entropy—the loss of all vitality and all centers of energy. A horizontal map, rooted in earth's surface (and, by extension, in the history of the physical universe), must take the potential risks and vicissitudes of earth's surface seriously.

For human beings today, the context for this warning is not principally remote future natural events: a new Ice Age, the sun "going nova," or the "entropization" of the entire universe. There is instead a possibility more menacing and immediate, one brought on by our own actions. If we are serious about the risks of history and wish to use the horizontal map to envision the future in a collective, transindividual manner, we must confront the vision of earthly life's total annihilation through nuclear war. This undermines the plausibility of all positive evolutionary visions of the future. Any model of the future, whether individual or collective, must compete with this haunting, fearful scenario. The picture of total future annihilation threatens every individual attempt to come to terms with death. It threatens our capacity to envision a future in continuity with the present. It robs us of the security that assumes a world that will continue as a human, lively world even when I as an individual will no longer be present to enjoy it.

What kind of spiritual and psychological impact does the nuclear threat have for me, for all of us today? This question has been explored by Robert Lifton in *The Broken Connection*. Lifton believes that the nuclear image makes it all but impossible for human beings today to reestablish the lost connection between living and dying.[5] The need for religious symbolism is great, but Lifton stresses how inadequate most symbolism is to guarantee security and hope against the background threat of nuclear catastrophe. Imagine, for instance, a future with a crowded heaven but a ruined, poisoned, and depopulated earth. This is surely a counter-image against which to measure the plausibility of any myth of cosmic evolution. The vision of nuclear annihilation demonstrates how pointless it is to evoke the horizontal model in an exclusively hopeful yet historical mode, without confronting the negative side of history and the future.

But it reveals also the limits of the traditional vertical model. Paradise is meant to be a place of bliss—yet the dead eternal inhabitants of such a realm, abiding high above the devastated landscape left by a nuclear holocaust, would be overwhelmed with grief. At least, we feel, they *ought* to grieve for the murdered earth—to mourn for what can only be described as an ultimate act of "petulant, deliberate blasphemy."[6] And what would divide the hopelessness of life upon such a dying earth from the despair of Dante's Hell?

Now that I have raised this dreadful vision so explicitly, is it possible to overcome its terror? Can I formulate an alternative of the future adequate to challenge this soul-destroying imagery? Lifton is pessimistic on this score. Christians who wish to see in the nuclear image the fulfillment of biblical prophecy do no justice to the horror of the possibility and generally assume that they will remain untouched by the massive suffering and death. I cannot follow their thinking on this question, nor can I claim to provide an alternative complete counter-myth of hope. But I believe that the spiral model of life map might offer some help, for it operates with a more complex understanding of time than does the more conventional horizontal, historical model.

For the spiral model of a life map, the loop backward was a rebuilding of the schematizations that constituted my past. I gained, in the backward action, a second past, a past remembered but this time remembered in a more inclusive manner, more deeply than the first past, which was the past of ordinary consciousness. From this vantage point, this place of return, the future too will needs appear rather differently. It will not be seen stretching out in a flat straight line ahead of me, a projection of what is already known and experienced. Just as the past I thought I knew turned out to be a screen memory for the unthematized, unschematized past, so too the future that I assumed I was to possess dissolves. On the one hand, my individual existence takes on that circular wholeness and completeness which excludes dependence upon the future to give it meaning and worth. I receive a sense of meaning from what is now and has been, and therefore I no longer demand that the future provide this for me. But at the same time, the schematized future I had built up for myself is as undermined as the schematized past I thought I possessed. The future opens, becomes a sphere of transformation rather than of repeated past and present experience. Therefore the I who begins the new forward section of the spiral's loop is no longer the same I who began to reflect backward. Or rather, just as I can speak of the redemption of the past, I can re-vision the future so that it becomes the realm of God's redemption and not merely of my horizontal journey through time.

What happens when this mode of individual life map is perceived as a symbol of a much greater pattern? The linear flow of history becomes a spiral, circular movement encompassing all things, returning them to their place of origin in God. For this process, a label such as evolution or an imagery of horizontal progress is much too simple and basically misleading. "Evolution" is a natural process, "progress" a series of human acts. The image I am suggesting denies both these possibilities: redemption, at this universal level just as at the personal level, is primarily the act of the God who redeems in Christ. Here I may cite again the example of Augustine, who ended his autobiography —which conforms to our spiral model—not with his conversion or his mother's death (book 9), nor with his current state of soul (book 10), but with a return to the creation.[7] Augustine saw his individual life map as indeed a living symbol of God's greatest and most primordial action, an action prior to time and therefore encompassing all possible times. Here—whatever Augustine's vision of history elsewhere—the horizontal model of linear development is irrelevant.

Given this pattern, this circular inclusive reality, the future to which baptism's imagery points is not, then, the future of my own individual death: at least, not my death understood in isolation from all other events, spiritual and biological. Nor is it any longer an an eschatological end flattened out into a horizontal, chronological cosmic point B. It is not to be conceived as a system of goal-directed evolution or as any other strictly historically imaginable future. The true consummation lies in the fulfillment of the circle, in God's power to create both pattern and wholeness out of the immense diversity of all that is, and in spite of all evil. Even the utmost limits of imaginable catastrophe could not reach farther than God's presence, his power to encompass what he creates. This fulfillment will belong to God and to that hidden, resurrected self which is hid with God in Christ until the circle is completed. And although language such as "until" may be a requirement from where I am, in God—according to this imagery—there is no real "before," "during," or "after."

The meanings for individual life-mapping I apprehend in baptismal imagery cannot isolate the individual and his or her existence entirely from this all-encompassing pattern. Baptism is in itself not the final consummation, the wholeness of the circle, even for my own single life map. Yet its imagery is critically important, as the marker at the beginning and the place to which I return. It can help me to envision the redemption of the past without necessarily accepting the myth of the fresh start and all its consequences. Baptism's imagery is a place which contains within itself the hidden reference to this cosmic consummation and closure as well as to my own individual death. In this exploration, I have tried to apprehend it as such a landmark in spiritual geography. It is or can become a place in my own personal life map, because above all it gives me a connecting link between my own identity and that of Christ. I have suggested various ways in which baptismal imagery can function toward this goal, depending on which model of life map one wishes to use. Through this exploration of one point in spiritual geography, I hope that others—and not only the dying—can say together with the East African convert, "I go now to him whom I saw in baptism."

Notes

Chapter 1: Adult Faith and Life-Mapping

1. Karl Barth, *The Word of God and the Word of Man* (Harper & Row, 1957), p. 34.

Chapter 2: Baptismal Imagery and Christian Experience

1. Rudolf Schnackenburg, *Baptism in the Thought of St. Paul,* p. 157. (Full facts of publication, when not given in the Notes, may be found in the Bibliography.)

2. "Death with Christ" and birth from "water and the Spirit" together have struck many scholars as closer to the language of Hellenistic mystery-piety than the other New Testament ideas. Earlier attempts to make an absolute division between Hebraic and Hellenistic elements in early Christianity have not worn well, nor is the possible association with mystery cults very helpful to understand the roots of baptism. Nevertheless, the sense of direct experiential identification with a deity, a supposed hallmark of mystery-cult piety, could be very close to what Paul expressed. More plausibly, it may have been exactly how some of his converts heard his words on baptism. As for the image of watery spiritual birth, this too seemed to speak to the widespread Hellenistic yearning for transcendence of death and matter, a yearning met by a variety of mystery cults and gnostic sects. Therefore, scholars often seem burdened by a duty to show specifically how Paul's conception differs from that of mystery piety, how it is thoroughly rooted in the Jewish sense of corporate personality rather than in the Hellenistic hope for ontological identification of believer and deity.

3. Schnackenburg, p. 126.

4. G. R. Beasley-Murray, *Baptism in the New Testament,* p. 273.

5. See Bibliography for works by Aland and Jeremias on this historical question.

6. Those who wish a detailed discussion of just these matters may consult Rudolf Schnackenburg's *Baptism in the Thought of St. Paul* or J. Christiaan Beker's *Paul the Apostle: The Triumph of God in Life and Thought* (Fortress Press, 1980).

7. Schnackenburg, pp. 137ff.

8. Beker, *Paul the Apostle.* This work stresses Paul's commitment to the Jewish apocalyptic framework of "unrealized" eschatology.

9. Ibid., p. 273.

10. Specifically, the baptismal passage in Romans uses the past tense for all the death language, the subjunctive for "we too might walk," and the future tense for all the resurrection references: i.e., "We shall also live with him" and "We shall certainly be united with him in a resurrection like his." As we have seen, Paul angrily rejected arguments that seemed to depend on "resurrection now," on a realized eschatology of baptism.

The letters to the Colossians and Ephesians, on the other hand, confidently assert resurrection as the *current* status of the baptized Christian (Col. 2:12; Eph. 2:6). Is this grammatical anomaly a matter of context or a central difference over a major theological issue? Perhaps Paul wrote this way because at Colossae the problem was quite different from that of Corinth (we know that he never wrote letters in a vacuum; there was always some problem to be addressed). Or is it virtually impossible that he would ever write in a "resurrection now" style, precisely because unrealized eschatology was intrinsic to his thought and hope?

11. For example, Reginald Fuller in *Made, Not Born* represents this position.

12. Beker, p. 233.

13. Even though the four canonical Gospels are in no way biographies of Jesus of Nazareth, they provide a good deal of information about him: for example, that Jesus was baptized by John. If we had only Paul's letters, we would never have known this.

14. Scholars have debated whether, and to what degree, the portrait of Saul/Paul in Acts is historical—i.e., if the Paul who wrote Romans underwent an experience essentially the same as what the author of Acts claims for him. Ironically, Christian ideals of conversion derive from the Acts narrative far more than from Paul's letters, and some advocates of believers' baptism use this account to make "conversion experience" precede baptism.

15. One scholarly context for debate on this was Bultmann's idea that passages such as "born of water and the Spirit" were the additions of a "sacramentalist" editor of the (nonsacramental) original text. This

suggestion was surely based in part on Bultmann's own antisacramental form of Protestantism. See Rudolf Bultmann, *Theology of the New Testa ment,* vol. 2 (Charles Scribner's Sons, 1955), p. 58.

16. Quoted in Hamman, *Baptism: Ancient Liturgies and Patristic Texts,* p. 64.

17. Quoted in A. Field, *From Darkness to Life,* p. 190.

18. It is found after the crucifixion, when the body of Jesus is pierced in the side by one of the soldiers "and at once there came out blood and water" (John 19:34). Very likely the water that flows here is an allusion to baptism, the blood to the Lord's Supper. Raymond Brown, *Commentary on the Gospel According to John,* Anchor Bible (Doubleday & Co., 1970), p. 951.

Chapter 3: From Imagery to Application

1. Clifford Geertz, *The Interpretation of Cultures* (Basic Books, 1973), p. 90.

2. A work that discusses religion as worldview and deals with this problem is Thomas Luckmann's *Invisible Religion: The Problem of Religion in Modern Society* (Macmillan Co., 1967).

3. Anthony Wallace, "Mazeway Resynthesis: A Biocultural Theory of Religious Inspiration," *Transactions of the New York Academy of Sciences* 18 (1956):631–632.

4. Two thinkers who take this latter position are R. D. Laing, *The Politics of Experience* (Ballantine Books, 1967), and Ernest Becker, *The Denial of Death* (Free Press, 1973).

5. *The Biographical Process: Studies in the History and Psychology of Religion,* ed. by Frank E. Reynolds and Donald Capps (Mouton Publishers, 1976).

6. Augustine, *Confessions* (New American Library, 1963), VII. 9.

7. See for example, Oscar Cullmann's essay, "Immortality of the Soul or Resurrection of the Dead?" in Krister Stendahl, ed., *Immortality and Resurrection* (Macmillan Co., 1965).

8. Rudolf Bultmann, "The New Testament and Mythology" in *Kerygma and Myth,* ed. by Hans W. Bartsch (Harper & Row, 1961).

9. One good criticism of Bultmann's solution is that he seems to assume that terms such as decision, faith, and obedience are intrinsically free from any worldview and can mean essentially the same thing to "mythic" Hellenistic readers of Paul's letters and to Heideggerian "modern man." This criticism is found in Paul Ricoeur, *The Conflict of Interpretations: Essays on Hermeneutics* (Northwestern University Press, 1974), "Preface to Bultmann." For the rest of the demythologizing debate, see Hans W. Bartsch, ed., *Kerygma and Myth.*

Chapter 4: Three Patterns of Life Maps

1. See F. E. Reynolds and D. Capps, *The Biographical Process* (ch. 3, note 5).

2. James Olney, *Metaphors of Self: The Meaning of Autobiography* (Princeton University Press, 1972), p. 44.

3. William Spengemann, *The Forms of Autobiography: Episodes in the History of a Literary Genre* (Yale University Press, 1980), p. xv.

4. John Bunyan, *The Pilgrim's Progress* (New American Library, 1981), p. 17.

5. Ibid., p. 19.

6. Ibid., p. 148.

7. Ibid., pp. 57–61.

8. Louisa M. Alcott, *Little Women* (Whitman Publishing Co., 1955), ch. 8.

9. Bunyan, p. 113.

10. Rudolf Bultmann, "New Testament and Mythology" (ch. 3, note 8), p. 4.

11. Dante Alighieri, *The Divine Comedy,* tr. by John Ciardi (New American Library, 1970), Paradiso, Canto III:64–87.

12. Ibid., Inferno, Cantos XIII–XVII.

13. Ibid., Paradiso, Canto XXXIII:85–87.

14. Augustine, *Confessions,* tr. by Rex Warner (New American Library, 1963), II. 4.

15. Ibid., IV. 6.

16. Olney, p. 270.

17. Such theories apply to literary autobiography, not to what are called "memoirs." We generally read autobiographical accounts of Watergate with questions of historical accuracy in mind, rather than for the light Nixon, Dean, Liddy, et al. shed on the human condition as such.

18. C. S. Lewis, *The Pilgrim's Regress* (Bantam Books, 1981), pp. 174–175.

19. Lewis's explanation of the Mappa Mundi in the Preface, pp. xv–xvi, makes this clear.

20. In the Preface to the revised edition. Ibid., p. vii.

Chapter 5: The Horizontal Life Map and the Myth of the Fresh Start

1. "The point about the melting pot . . . is that it did not happen," state Nathan Glazer and Daniel P. Moynihan, in the preface to *Beyond the Melting Pot* (M.I.T. Press, 1963). The other point is that this had to be stated so emphatically and controversially.

2. Gail Sheehy, *Passages: Predictable Crises of Adult Life* (E. P. Dutton & Co., 1974), ch. 25, "Renewal."

3. Ibid., p. 122.

4. Ibid., p. 126.

5. Ibid., p. 251.

6. Ibid., p. 243.

7. Try as I may, I can't recall the exact name of the narrator, only the tale and the occasion. Perhaps it's just as well.

8. See, for example, Flo Conway and Jim Siegelman, *Snapping: America's Epidemic of Sudden Personality Change* (J. B. Lippincott Co., 1978).

Chapter 6: Vertical Life Maps and the Places of Baptism

1. Charles T. Tart in *Transpersonal Psychologies,* ed. by Charles T. Tart (Harper & Row, 1975), p. 6.

2. Daniel Goleman, *The Varieties of Meditative Experience* (E. P. Dutton & Co., 1977), part 1.

3. G. Alexander, "William James, the Sick Soul, and the Negative Dimensions of Consciousness: A Partial Critique of Transpersonal Psychology," *Journal of the American Academy of Religion* 48 (June 1980): 191–205.

4. James Hillman, *The Dream and the Underworld* (Harper & Row, 1979), p. 16.

5. Ibid., p. 90.

6. Ibid., p. 32.

7. As do the editors of *The New Oxford Annotated Bible* (Oxford University Press, 1973), p. 1367.

8. See particularly Simone Weil, *Waiting for God* (Harper & Row, 1973).

Chapter 7: The Spiral Life Map

1. James Olney, *Metaphors of Self* (ch. 4, note 2), p. 204.

2. Ibid., pp. 196–197.

3. C. S. Lewis, *A Grief Observed* (Bantam Books, 1976), pp. 12, 20.

4. F. C. Bartlett, *Remembering: A Study in Experimental and Social Psychology* (London: Cambridge University Press, 1932), pp. 118ff.

5. Ibid., pp. 180–181.

6. Roger Brown and James Kulik, "Flashbulb Memories," in *Memory Observed: Remembering in Natural Contexts,* ed. by Ulric Neisser (W. H. Freeman and Co., 1982), p. 24.

7. Ibid., pp. 25–26.

8. Ulric Neisser, "Snapshots or Benchmarks?" in *Memory Observed,* p. 45.

9. Ibid., p. 47.

10. D. Rubin, "Very Long-Term Memory for Prose and Verse," in *Memory Observed,* pp. 299–310.

11. A. R. Luria, "The Mind of a Mnemonist," in *Memory Observed,* pp. 382–389.

12. Sigmund Freud, *Three Case Histories* (Collier Books, 1963), pp. 221ff.

13. Ibid., pp. 201ff.

14. The movie *Blow-Up* used this "innocent photographer" plot device.

15. Erik Erikson, *Childhood and Society* (W. W. Norton & Co., 1963), ch. 7, "Eight Ages of Man," esp. pp. 247–251.

16. Erik Erikson, *Young Man Luther* (W. W. Norton & Co., 1962), pp. 206–209. The relevance of this theory to the historical Luther is beside the point here. See the essays in Roger Johnson (ed.), *Psychohistory and Religion: The Case of Young Man Luther* (Fortress Press, 1977).

17. James Fowler, *Stages of Faith: The Psychology of Human Development and the Quest for Meaning* (Harper & Row, 1981), pp. 92–93.

18. Ibid., chs. 18–21.

19. Ibid., Fig. 5.2, p. 289.

20. Ibid., p. 264.

21. Ibid., pp. 264–265.

22. Ibid., p. 264.

23. John McDargh, *Psychoanalytic Object Relations Theory and the Study of Religion: On Faith and the Imaging of God* (University Press of America, 1983), p. 98.

24. Ibid., p. 99.

25. Quoted in Philip Rieff, *Freud: The Mind of the Moralist* (Doubleday & Co., 1959), p. 358.

Chapter 8: The Redemption of the Past

1. I am aware of the current controversy over Freud's abandonment of the seduction theory—i.e., the view that his patients had actually been the victims of sexual abuse by their parents. It seems that at times Freud was quite willing to speak of "real seduction." But it is fair to say that what interested Freud is not the level of family dynamics but interior construction of the events, their emotional impact in terms of the psychic state of the child. See "The Wolf Man" in his *Three Case Histories* (Collier Books, 1963).

2. James Fowler, *Stages of Faith* (ch. 7, note 17), p. 264.

3. Edward Robinson, *The Original Vision: A Study of the Religious Experience of Childhood* (Seabury Press, 1983), p. 44.

4. Ibid., p. 96.

5. See M. Scott Peck, *The Road Less Traveled* (Simon & Schuster, 1980), p. 236.

6. John McDargh, *Psychoanalytic Object Relations Theory and the Study of Religion* (ch. 7, note 23), p. 48.

7. Such a contrast can be made without reference to the church affiliation of any of the theorists. However, McDargh's interpretation may well help explain why Fowler's ideas are so popular among Roman Catholic religious educators, and also among those Protestants for whom a "continuity" view of nature and grace prevails.

Chapter 9: Baptismal Imagery and the Future

1. See Philippe Aries, *The Hour of Our Death* (Alfred A. Knopf, 1981).

2. Oscar Cullmann, "Immortality of the Soul or Resurrection of the Dead?" in Krister Stendahl, ed., *Immortality and Resurrection* (ch. 3, note 7).

3. Emil Brunner, *Eternal Hope* (London: Lutterworth Press, 1954), takes this approach.

4. This model of eschatology as cosmic evolution is popular in and out of Christianity in the twentieth century. Its scientific status, its universalism, and its ambiguity as to whether evolution is something "we do" or something that "just happens" have all been extensively debated.

5. Robert J. Lifton, *The Broken Connection: On Death and the Continuity of Life* (Simon & Schuster, 1979), Part 3, "Death and History—the Nuclear Image."

6. Ibid., p. 344. Lifton is quoting Loren Eiseley here.

7. Augustine, *Confessions* XI. 3ff.

Bibliography
of Christian Initiation
Literature

Aland, Kurt. *Did the Early Church Baptize Infants?* Westminster Press. 1963.

Barth, Karl. *The Teaching of the Church Regarding Baptism.* Tr. by E. A. Payne. Toronto: Macmillan, 1948.

Beasley-Murray, George R. *Baptism in the New Testament.* St. Martin's Press, 1961.

Field, A. *From Darkness to Light: What It Meant to Become a Christian in the Early Church.* Servant Books, 1978.

Flemington, W. F. *The New Testament Doctrine of Baptism.* London: SPCK, 1953.

Hamman, Andre. *Baptism: Ancient Liturgies and Patristic Texts.* Ed. by Thomas Halton. Alba House, 1967.

Jeremias, Joachim. *Infant Baptism in the First Four Centuries.* Tr. by David Cairns. Westminster Press, 1961.

Made, Not Born: New Perspectives on Christian Initiation and the Catechumenate. Ed. by the Murphy Center for Liturgical Research. University of Notre Dame Press, 1976.

"Putting on Christ." *Liturgy,* vol. 4, no. 1 (Winter 1983).

Schnackenburg, Rudolf. *Baptism in the Thought of St. Paul: A Study in Pauline Theology.* Tr. by G. R. Beasley-Murray. Herder & Herder, 1964.

Wainwright, Geoffrey. *Christian Initiation.* John Knox Press, 1969.

Werner, Martin. *The Formation of Christian Dogma: An Historical Study . . . Rewritten in Shortened Form by the Author. . . .* Tr. by S. G. F. Brandon. Harper & Brothers, 1957.